HOW TO
COMMUNICATE
With Your Spanish
& Asian Employees

A Translation Guide for Small Business Owners—
With Companion CD-ROM

Kimberley Hicks, B.A., B.Ed.

How to Communicate with Your Spanish & Asian Employees: A Translation
Guide for Small Business Owners—With Companion CD-ROM

Atlantic Publishing Group, Inc. Copyright © 2005
1210 SW 23rd Place
Ocala, Florida 34474
800-541-1336
352-622-5836–Fax

www.atlantic-pub.com–Web site
sales@atlantic-pub.com–E-mail

SAN Number :268-1250

International Standard Book Number: 0-910627-39-8

Library of Congress Cataloging-in-Publication Data

Hicks, Kimberley.
How to communicate with your Spanish & Asian employees : a translation guide for small business owners, with companion CD-ROM / Kimberley Hicks.
p. cm.
Includes index.
ISBN 0-910627-39-8 (alk. paper)
1. Small business--United States--Management. 2. Small business--United States--Employees. 3. Business communication--Cross-cultural studies. 4. Spanish language--Glossaries, vocabularies, etc. 5. Chinese language--Glossaries, vocabularies, etc. 6. English language--Glossaries, vocabularies, etc. I. Title.

HD62.7.H53 2004
658.3'0089'68073--dc22

                          2004013985

Printed in the United States

Book cover, layout and design by Meg Buchner of Megadesign
www.mega-designs.com • e-mail: megadesn@mchsi.com

Table of Contents

Chapter 5   The Workplace

Appendix A   Job Interviews and Employment Applications

Appendix B   Independance Days

Common Workplace Terminology

ENDNOTES & SOURCES

introduction

> **" It's a small world after all. "**
> —Walt Disney

"It's a small world after all." Walt Disney made some money with that sentiment. But as cliché as it has become, it is undeniably the case in business. With relaxed trade barriers and the creation of economic alliances such as the North American Free Trade Agreement (NAFTA), the European Union (EU) and the Association of Southeast Asian Nations (ASEAN), the global market is virtually an open door to American business. Convenient air travel, telecommunications innovations and the advent of "overnight delivery" anywhere in the world allow businesses access to an incredibly diverse network of international customers, suppliers, partners and employees. But the same factors that drive big business and multinational corporations can be difficult for small-business owners and operators.

Today's small-business owners and managers are faced with a myriad of challenges to survive and succeed: coping with the rising costs of labor, production, distribution and advertising; keeping up with ultra-fast technological advancements; and struggling to maintain a competitive edge, to name a few. One of the toughest challenges of modern management is understanding and navigating the complexities of an increasingly diverse workforce.

In order to be successful in today's marketplace, employers must be able to recruit and competently manage a staff with potentially many different backgrounds, value systems and languages. Almost 18 percent of people in the United States over age five speak a language other than English at home, and another 8 percent are "limited-English proficient." The ability to effectively communicate with all employees is critical to reaping the many rewards of a diverse workforce. For many small-business owners, that reality requires a new way of thinking about work, people and communication.

Almost 18 percent of people in the United States over age five speak a language other than English.

The purpose of this book is to help small-business owners and employers do just that: learn to communicate comfortably and successfully with employees whose mother tongue is not English. The face of America's workforce is multinational: the United States is home to people of virtually every country in the world. It is highly unlikely that you will not encounter—and hire—a job applicant, or many, whose roots originated elsewhere.

This manual will focus specifically on communicating with workers from Spanish-speaking and Asian countries, primarily because these groups represent the fastest growing segment of the American population and labor force.[1] Obviously, these two groups include a multitude of nationalities, but for the purposes of this book, the term "Hispanic American" will be used to denote persons of Spanish-speaking origins, and "Asian American" will refer to people from Asia, South Asia and the Pacific Islands.

Generally speaking, references to these groups of workers will denote "foreign-born" Americans, that is, immigrants, because it is assumed that working-age people born and educated in the United States can speak English and have grown up fairly saturated with mainstream

The ability to effectively communicate with all employees is critical to reaping the many rewards of a diverse workforce.

"American" culture. While standard management issues and practices and effective communication are relevant to all employer/employee relationships, meeting the specific challenges presented by working with people of different cultures and first languages is the primary purpose of this book.

In meeting this purpose, we have devised a two-part handbook for small businesses, applicable for use in a professional office environment, the food service and hospitality industry or retail arena. The first part of this manual is intended to be a resource guide for employers. It will discuss what the multinational workforce looks like in this age of "globalism." It will define what is meant by "culture";

what constitutes "effective communication," and demonstrate how to apply this knowledge to your managing and leadership skills. The second part of this book is a glossary and phrase book designed to help your employees learn basic English conversation and language they may encounter in the workplace.

CHAPTER 1

The Workforce and Diversity

"All history is a record of the power of minorities, and of minorities of one."
—Ralph Waldo Emerson

The Face of the Multinational Workforce

Note: *The U.S. Census Bureau refers to race in many of its demographic statistics, but points out that it does so according to self-identification of respondents' racial identity. It defines the word "race" for census purposes as "racial, national origin and socio-cultural groups," not a set of biological characteristics. Census documents also point out that people of Hispanic origins may be of any "race" (White, Black, Native American, Asian/Pacific Islander). This book will refer to different groups in terms of "ethnicity" rather than race, an ethnic group being comprised of people who share a similar national or geographic origin, culture, language and customs.*

For the sake of brevity, we have opted to use the terms "Hispanic American" and "Asian American" to distinguish these groups of immigrants, with the full awareness that they comprise many different nationalities, cultures and dialects and that it is preferable to refer to a person's country of origin. Examples of Hispanic nationalities are: Mexican, Puerto Rican (American), Central American (e.g., Cuban, Dominican), South American (e.g., Colombian, Venezuelan), Other Latino group. Asian Americans include: Chinese, Taiwanese, Filipino, Korean, Vietnamese, Japanese, Malaysian, Asian Indian, Native Hawaiian, Samoan and Pacific Islander, Other Asian group (e.g., Thai, Laotian, Cambodian).

As of July 2002, the total population of Hispanic Americans reached 38.8 million, making that group the largest minority group in the United States.

The number of both Hispanic Americans and Asian Americans living in the United States is projected to double in the next two decades. As of July 2002, the total population of Hispanic Americans reached 38.8 million, making that group the largest minority group in the United States. Asian Americans totaled 12.5 million, with that group showing the highest rate of population growth at 9 percent.[2]

In the same year, nearly 12 percent of Americans—or 32.5 million people—were born in another country.[3] More than half of the foreign-born population came from Mexico, Central America and South America, and over a quarter from Asia. Of all foreign-born Americans, more than one in three are naturalized citizens and nearly 7 percent are unemployed (compared to 6.1 percent of native-born Americans).

These figures translate into a huge potential workforce available for savvy entrepreneurs to recruit. It is important, though, to recognize and be aware of some of the issues that arise with a team of diverse employees, both from the perspective of the small-business owner or manager and the employees themselves.

Having lived and worked in Japan for two years, and in the far north for another four, I have experienced some of the trials and tribulations encountered by people who arrive in a new country as a visible minority with nothing more than a rudimentary ability to communicate in the local language and the desire to succeed in their new home.

While some of us uproot and immerse ourselves in another country and culture temporarily, most immigrants do so permanently. For many, especially refugees, there is no going back to the familiar place called home. Immigrants are faced with the huge challenge (and often hardship) of having to navigate nearly every aspect of their daily lives in a new and unfamiliar way.

There are the practical hurdles such as finding a house or apartment, finding a job, learning the transportation system (if there is one), getting a driver's license and Social Security number, securing medical and child care, buying groceries (which may be strange and new), paying bills, conducting business at the immigration office, bank, post office, social agencies, etc. To accomplish all of these things successfully, there is an imperative to learn to communicate in a new language. If an immigrant arrives in his or her new country with existing family or a community support network in place, the transition can be easier. But for those arriving on their own, the adjustment is daunting indeed.

In addition to these obstacles, immigrants often confront the most insurmountable barrier: intolerance. Despite the "cultural capital" that many immigrants bring to their new country—fluency in another language (or several), cultural and geographic knowledge, the courage and resilience necessary to start a new life, and often considerable work experience, specialized skills and education—many immigrants experience being dismissed as "foreign," "uneducated" and "un-American."

Hispanic Americans employed in the service industry:
22.1%

Many foreign-born and native-born minorities struggle to find decent-paying jobs with safe working conditions and end up with temporary, minimum-wage jobs with long hours and no health benefits, or unemployed: 46 percent of immigrants work for less than $7.50 per hour compared to 28 percent of all workers, and only 26 percent have job-based health insurance.[4] According to the most recent census data available (2002), 22.1 percent of the Hispanic American civilian labor force was employed in service industry occupations, such as fast food, and 8 percent were unemployed.[5] Almost an equal number (21.8 percent) were below the poverty line, compared to 8 percent of non-Hispanic whites and a national poverty rate of 12.1 percent.[6]

The numbers are somewhat different for Asian Americans: only 10 percent of whom were below the poverty line in 2002. Occupational statistics for this group were separated by gender, but they still show fewer Asian Americans than Hispanic Americans occupying service jobs: 12.4 percent for men and under 17 percent for women. The unemployment rate for Asian Americans was 6 percent (compared to 5 percent for non-Hispanic whites).[7]

The face of the American labor force is not one color: it has multiple shades and reflects innumerable experiences, skills, languages and abilities, and it offers unlimited potential.

Diversity: Benefits and Challenges

" Honest differences are often a healthy sign of progress."
—Mahatma Gandhi

Most entrepreneurs are, by necessity, propelled by their bottom line. Decisions need to be made to ensure profitability or you are out of business. But behind the numbers on the balance sheet remain the principal factors that determine success or failure: your employees. If you have employees, you also have all of the issues and concerns that go with managing them: payroll, training, scheduling, evaluating performance, absenteeism, incentives, feedback, conflict, labor laws, insurance, discipline, and the list goes on.

When you have employees from different parts of the world, with different cultural values and speaking different languages, you are challenged with the usual management issues and then some. Making diversity work to the advantage of the business presents management with the multiple challenges of being able to work successfully with the daily difficulties of those various personalities and backgrounds (coordinating a cohesive team, resolving conflict, communicating well), balancing individual needs with those of the entire team and fostering a work environment that values all of those elements and overcomes resistance to change, all of which may require considerable effort from everyone in the company.

However, in tandem with the challenges, diversity also offers employers a potential wealth of benefits. Some researchers of diversity in the workplace have determined benefits to include increased productivity, heightened creativity and problem-solving ability, increasing market-ing capabilities and retention of business, creating the largest possible talent pool for recruitment, boosting morale, becoming an employer of choice and fewer lawsuits.[8] The following list describes in more detail several ways in which an inclusive environment can lead to a competi-tive advantage.

- **Better problem-solving.** Managing and working with people of disparate backgrounds allows you to bring together a team that can solve problems and creatively move the company forward. Looking at an issue from a completely different point of view and fielding questions you may never have thought about are immensely useful in the brainstorming and problem-solving process.

- **Increased productivity.** People tend to work harder in a workplace where everyone feels valued and included. Morale is higher and people are willing and eager to do their best for the common good of the company. Opportunities for success not only keep people in an organization, but encourage them to perform.

- **Increased marketing opportunities.** You will reach a wider client base because of your employees' knowledge of and experience with habits, preferences and trends of other cultures. Consumers who feel their needs and experiences are understood and reflected by a company's workforce will express their approval, comfort level and appreciation through repeat business.

- **Increased talent pool.** Drawing from all available human resources increases your likelihood of finding the right person for the job. When you expand your talent search from the traditional job networks and schools, you discover that there are qualified, hard-working and enthusiastic candidates to be found everywhere. Searching for skills at a community level may also positively impact the educational system: if you have a need for a specific skill set and can potentially employ a number of people in a community, curriculum requirements may evolve to meet the employment need and enhance the "employability" of future job-seekers. It's a winning cycle.

- **Enhanced reputation.** Companies that are known to hire particular groups attract more people from that group, particularly the best. Talented people from any group expect fair treatment and equal opportunity for advancement and they are eager to recommend an employer who rewards performance. Employees are more apt to remain loyal when they know their boss is respectful of and sympathetic to their individual needs and styles.

- **Increased economic contribution.** Employers who hire and retain people from local areas help build communities by contributing to the tax base and the social fabric. Employees who live and work in the same general locale tend to shop there too. Shorter commuting times allow people to spend more time with their families and participate in neighborhood activities. More tax dollars, in theory, stay in the community for improvements to schools, transit systems, parks, roads, etc.

- **Decreased litigation.** If you hire a diverse team and make genuine efforts to support each member, you will theoretically reduce your likelihood of being sued for discrimination. People sue their employers because they feel their workplace is a hostile environment, whether it is openly so (racial slurs, offensive jokes or aggressive behavior) or the hostility is more subtle but equally discriminating (being passed over for promotion, earning lower wages than others in equivalent jobs, being ignored in meetings or avoided at social events).

CHAPTER 2

Legal Issues

" A law is valuable not because it is law, but because there is right in it. "
—Henry Ward Beecher

Employment Legislation

Most of the employment laws in the United States revolve around Title VII of *The Civil Rights Act of 1964* and *1991* which prohibits discrimination based on race, color, religion, sex and national origin. Under the Act, it is illegal to recruit, hire, promote, demote or fire anyone based on where the person comes from, their accent, level of English fluency (unless proven to be critical to the job), skin color, hair texture, facial features or marriage to or association with someone of a particular group. The Act also protects workers from a hostile work environment which allows harassment of any kind to take place including, but not limited to, racial slurs, insulting jokes and other offensive behavior. It is illegal to threaten or retaliate against employees who do lodge a complaint of discrimination.

Title VII applies to employers and small businesses of 15 or more employees, including part-time and temporary workers. Independent contractors are not considered employees because they generally do not appear on the regular company payroll. The *Age Discrimination in Employment Act* enacted in 1967 protects workers over 40 from discriminatory practices in businesses of 20 or more employees. The 1990 *Americans with Disabilities Act* added people with disabilities to the list of qualified employees against which it is illegal to discriminate in a workplace of 15 or more staff.

In 2002, almost
30,000
racial
discrimination
charges
were filed with
the Equal Employment
Commission.

Larger businesses with 100 or more employees, or 50 or more employees plus federal contracts totaling a minimum of $50,000, must file an annual Employment Information Report (EEO-1) with a breakdown of employee numbers by race and gender.[9] (A sample of this form can be found at the end of this chapter.)

If your business does not fall under the Title VII criteria, you are not legally compelled to follow the Act. However, the costs of not complying with Title VII can be high.

In 2002, the Equal Employment Opportunity Commission (EEOC), the federal agency which is in charge of enforcing civil rights laws, received 29,910 charges of racial-based discrimination (including more than 9,000 based on national origin). Of the total, the EEOC resolved over 33,000 charges—including some from previous years—that resulted in $81 million in benefits paid to complainants, not including any damages awarded through litigation!

The EEOC lists the following practices in which it is illegal to discriminate in any aspect of employment:

- Hiring and firing.

- Compensation, assignment and classification of employees.

- Transfer, promotion, layoff or recall.

- Job advertisements.

- Testing, training and internships.

- Recruitment.

- Benefits, pay, leave of absence and retirement plans.

- Retaliation for filing a charge of discrimination.

Employers are also required by law to clearly post notices advising employees of their rights in a clear and accessible manner. The EEOC points out that some state and municipal laws extend to protect against discrimination based on sexual orientation, marital status and political affiliation. The onus is on the employer to be aware of employment laws at the local level.[10]

Another aspect of the law that is worthy of note to business owners is the *Immigration Reform and Control Act of 1986*. Under the IRCA, employers are mandated to ensure that all employees are legally authorized to work in the country. It is an offense to require valid documents only from candidates or employees of a different national origin or "individuals who appear to be or sound foreign."[11] It is also a violation of the Act if employers impose citizenship requirements on employees or give hiring preference to U.S. citizens. As long as an individual is legally allowed to work in the United States (e.g., has a working visa or a green card) and is qualified for the job, employers cannot discriminate against him or her on the basis that he or she does not hold formal citizenship.

If passed, the Development, Relief, and Education for Alien Minors (DREAM) Act, could greatly impact the availability of employees.

The *Immigration Act of 1990* substantially changed the preferential ranking of people immigrating from how they were listed in the 1965 law. While the earlier Act gave priority to immigrants sponsored by U.S. citizens and permanent residents and focused on the reunification of family members (unmarried children under 21, spouses and siblings), the more recent law adds an economically driven priority and addresses immigration to the United States for purposes of employment. One of the new categories provides up to 10,000 visas a year to qualified immigrants who wish to enter the United States to establish a new commercial enterprise (defined as "any lawful business" that benefits the U.S. economy and creates full-time employment for at least ten lawfully employable people). "Qualified" refers to the requirement for foreign entrepreneurs to invest $1 million in the business enterprise, or $500,000 in targeted areas of high unemployment and a population greater than 20,000.[12]

New legislation pending in Congress may be of particular interest to business owners and entrepreneurs seeking a young and motivated talent pool. The *Development, Relief, and Education for Alien Minors (DREAM) Act* was introduced to the Senate in July 2003 as a joint effort of Republicans and Democrats to address federal barriers to higher education and work faced by children raised in the United States by parents without legal immigration status. The DREAM Act targets 65,000 students who have lived in the United States for at least five years and graduated from high school but can't apply for permanent resident status or state education benefits because of their parents' status. The new legislation would eliminate a federal provision that ties in-state tuition to immigration status and would grant students "of good moral character" a 6-year conditional permanent residency which could be totally permanent if they met at least one of the following requirements: graduating from or studying for at least two years at the college level, serving at least two years in the military, or completing 910 hours of volunteer community service.[13]

Proponents of the DREAM Act, including Senator Orrin Hatch (R-UT) and Senator Richard Durbin (D-IL) who tabled it, and another bi-partisan group behind a similar bill in the House known as the Student Adjustment Act, predict that the costs of the initial educational investment would be paid back within 3 to 4 years through increased taxes that would be paid by those who qualify and enter the workforce legally, as well as from lowering the potential costs to the criminal justice system (where it is presumed many of these students would end up without an opportunity to advance their skills and legally earn a living.)

Whether or not the motivation behind the legislation serves a purely economic agenda, it would open the door of opportunity to many young, talented and hardworking individuals who would otherwise be left in limbo and offers an equally valuable opportunity to large and small businesses to recruit a diverse American-educated workforce.

Major Lawsuits

Several high-profile class action lawsuits have been in the news recently, including potentially one of the largest civil rights suits in U.S. history against Wal-Mart. Although the company ranked number one in 2003 on Fortune Magazine's list of "America's Most Admired Companies," almost 1.6 million current and former female workers have filed a class action lawsuit alleging they were denied equal pay, promotions, managerial positions and training as male employees.[14] At this time, the case is still being examined by the California courts.

In January 2004, the New York City Police Department agreed to pay a $26.8 million settlement to approximately 12,000 minority police officers, predominantly Hispanic Americans, who charged that they were discriminated against, suffered harsher discipline than white officers, and were retaliated against for bringing complaints.[15]

Ten years ago, the restaurant chain Denny's lost two class action discrimination lawsuits and was forced to pay $54 million dollars in damages to employees and customers who charged that they were treated poorly based on race. Today the parent company, Atlantica Restaurant Group Inc., reports that one-quarter of its workforce and 32 percent of supervisory positions are held by minority groups. They also increased their contracts with minority suppliers from $0 in 1982 to $100 million in 2002.[16]

While larger companies can survive a discrimination lawsuit and incorporate positive changes to their employment practices in the aftermath, it is clear that the potential damages could quickly bankrupt a small business.

The Bottom Line

Entrepreneurs are simply those who understand that there is little difference between obstacle and opportunity and are able to turn both to their advantage.

—*Victor Kiam*

Other than potential legal costs of discrimination, there are other inherent costs to a company that does not reflect diversity in its workforce and business practices. There is a very real cost to losing staff: lost time and productivity, the expense of hiring temporary replacements, advertising for new permanent employees, the time and cost of interviewing and re-training, and possibly severance pay. There is also the cost to your corporate reputation that can seriously affect your balance sheet when customers decide to take their business elsewhere.

Certainly some small-business owners would say that it is difficult to accurately weigh the costs versus the benefits of diversity. To implement the necessary language and training programs and support networks in the diverse workplace to make it successful also requires time, effort and money. There are seemingly no concrete ways to measure, track and report the specific pay-offs of that investment, other than by the typical markers of personnel numbers.[17]

The biggest study to date on the business benefits of diversity was done in 2003 by the Massachusetts Institute of Technology's (MIT) Sloan School of Management. Researchers encountered a number of problems in the study that included reluctance among companies to have their diversity efforts examined in any detail, inconsistent methods of recordkeeping of diversity-related data, and fear of publicity and potential legal ramifications.[18] The overall conclusion, however, was that businesses should look beyond the hard numbers that are difficult to quantify and look toward effectively managing a staff to ensure that the more anecdotal benefits are enhanced.

Asian Americans will spend
$900 Billion
annually by 2007.

The growing demographic of diversity is certainly viewed by major American banks and auto manufacturers as a lucrative business opportunity. The buying power of Asian Americans is projected to increase from $296 billion in 2002 to $450 billion in the next five years. Even more dramatically, buying power of Hispanic Americans is expected to exceed $900 billion dollars by 2007.[19] Consequently, financial institutions such as Bank of America and JP Morgan Chase are launching marketing campaigns specifically targeted at these groups of consumers using multicultural "in-language" (e.g., Mandarin, Cantonese, Korean and Vietnamese) television, radio and print advertisements. Major banks in California, New York and New Jersey provide Asian-language automated teller machines, credit applications and brochures for clients who are more comfortable in their first language.

Similarly, major car makers—Nissan Motor Co., Toyota Motor Sales U.S.A., American Honda, General Motors and Ford Motor Company— are also targeting "consumers of color" through advertising media. All of the manufacturers' campaigns feature community involvement through diverse dealership-development programs and partnerships with community organizations.[20]

Rather than ignoring cultural diversity, big business is embracing the opportunity to tap into all facets of the consumer market. The current and projected returns should be attractive to small businesses as well.

Joint Reporting
Committee

• **Equal Employment
Opportunity Com-
mission**
• **Office of Federal
Contract Compli-
ance Programs (Labor)**

EQUAL EMPLOYMENT OPPORTUNITY

EMPLOYER INFORMATION REPORT EEO—1

Standard Form 100
(Rev. 4–92)
O.M.B. No. 3046–0007
EXPIRES 12/31/93
100–213

Section A—TYPE OF REPORT
Refer to instructions for number and types of reports to be filed.

1. Indicate by marking in the appropriate box the type of reporting unit for which this copy of the form is submitted (MARK ONLY ONE BOX).

(1) ☐ Single-establishment Employer Report

Multi-establishment Employer:
(2) ☐ Consolidated Report (Required)
(3) ☐ Headquarters Unit Report (Required)
(4) ☐ Individual Establishment Report (submit one for each establishment with 50 or more employees)
(5) ☐ Special Report

2. Total number of reports being filed by this Company (Answer on Consolidated Report only) _____

Section B—COMPANY IDENTIFICATION (To be answered by all employers)

	OFFICE USE ONLY
1. Parent Company	
a. Name of parent company (owns or controls establishment in item 2) omit if same as label	a.
Address (Number and street)	
	b.
City or town / State / ZIP code	c.
2. Establishment for which this report is filed. (Omit if same as label)	
a. Name of establishment	d.
Address (Number and street) / City or Town / County / State / ZIP code	e.
b. Employer Identification No. (IRS 9-DIGIT TAX NUMBER)	f.

c. Was an EEO–1 report filed for this establishment last year? ☐ Yes ☐ No

Section C—EMPLOYERS WHO ARE REQUIRED TO FILE (To be answered by all employers)

☐ Yes ☐ No 1. Does the entire company have at least 100 employees in the payroll period for which you are reporting?

☐ Yes ☐ No 2. Is your company affiliated through common ownership and/or centralized management with other entities in an enterprise with a total employment of 100 or more?

☐ Yes ☐ No 3. Does the company or any of its establishments (a) have 50 or more employees AND (b) is not exempt as provided by 41 CFR 60-1.5, AND either (1) is a prime government contractor or first-tier subcontractor, and has a contract, subcontract, or purchase order amounting to $50,000 or more, or (2) serves as a depository of Government funds in any amount or is a financial institution which is an issuing and paying agent for U.S. Savings Bonds and Savings Notes?

If the response to question C–3 is yes, please enter your Dun and Bradstreet identification number (if you have one): ☐☐☐☐☐☐☐☐☐

NOTE: If the answer is yes to questions 1, 2, or 3, complete the entire form, otherwise skip to Section G.

NSN 7540–00–180–6384

SF 100 Page 2

Section D—EMPLOYMENT DATA

Employment at this establishment—Report all permanent full-time and part-time employees including apprentices and on-the-job trainees unless specifically excluded as set forth in the instructions. Enter the appropriate figures on all lines and in all columns. Blank spaces will be considered as zeros.

JOB CATEGORIES		OVERALL TOTALS (SUM OF COL. B THRU K)	MALE					FEMALE				
			WHITE (NOT OF HISPANIC ORIGIN)	BLACK (NOT OF HISPANIC ORIGIN)	HISPANIC	ASIAN OR PACIFIC ISLANDER	AMERICAN INDIAN OR ALASKAN NATIVE	WHITE (NOT OF HISPANIC ORIGIN)	BLACK (NOT OF HISPANIC ORIGIN)	HISPANIC	ASIAN OR PACIFIC ISLANDER	AMERICAN INDIAN OR ALASKAN NATIVE
		A	B	C	D	E	F	G	H	I	J	K
Officials and Managers	1											
Professionals	2											
Technicians	3											
Sales Workers	4											
Office and Clerical	5											
Craft Workers (Skilled)	6											
Operatives (Semi-Skilled)	7											
Laborers (Unskilled)	8											
Service Workers	9											
TOTAL	10											
Total employment reported in previous EEO-1 report	11											

NOTE: Omit questions 1 and 2 on the Consolidated Report.

1. Date(s) of payroll period used: 2. Does this establishment employ apprentices?
       1 ☐ Yes   2 ☐ No

Section E—ESTABLISHMENT INFORMATION *(Omit on the Consolidated Report)*

1. What is the major activity of this establishment? (Be specific, i.e., manufacturing steel castings, retail grocer, wholesale plumbing supplies, title insurance, etc. Include the specific type of product or type of service provided, as well as the principal business or industrial activity.)

OFFICE USE ONLY

g.

Section F—REMARKS

Use this item to give any identification data appearing on last report which differs from that given above, explain major changes in composition or reporting units and other pertinent information.

Section G—CERTIFICATION *(See Instructions G)*

Check one   1 ☐ All reports are accurate and were prepared in accordance with the instructions (check on consolidated only)
      2 ☐ This report is accurate and was prepared in accordance with the instructions.

Name of Certifying Official	Title	Signature	Date

Name of person to contact regarding this report (Type or print)	Address (Number and Street)		

Title	City and State	ZIP Code	Telephone Number (Including Area Code)	Extension

All reports and information obtained from individual reports will be kept confidential as required by Section 709(e) of Title VII. WILLFULLY FALSE STATEMENTS ON THIS REPORT ARE PUNISHABLE BY LAW, U.S. CODE, TITLE 18, SECTION 1001.

CHAPTER **3**

Understanding Culture

" *No culture can live if it attempts to be exclusive.* "
—Mahatma Gandhi

Culture and Prejudice

In our society, "culture" typically refers to the arts—music, literature, painting, dance—and a sophisticated appreciation of those pursuits. Someone may be considered "cultured" if they frequent the opera or can discuss the themes of Shakespeare. Culture can also refer to cultivation (agriculture, horticulture) and the growth of organisms in a lab dish (bacterial culture).

For our purposes, culture will be defined as a shared set of beliefs and values of a particular group: the customs, practices and social behavior of a group of people connected by a common characteristic whether it is geographical, linguistic or historical. Our culture forms how we are raised; it informs how we view the rest of the world and our place in it. Our culture determines our perceptions of what constitutes truth, beauty, justice, quality, faith, humor, and so on. Culture dictates our ideas of status, concepts of time, use of space, manners and laws.

cul • ture (kulʼcher)
a shared set of beliefs and values of a particular group: the customs, practices and social behavior of a group of people connected by a common characteristic.

Our culture also determines how we distinguish ourselves as separate from "others." We divide ourselves into visible categories such as race (e.g., genetically similar characteristics) and gender, and into less obvious divisions such as nationality (our country of birth), class (our social and economic status), religion and sexual orientation. It is human instinct to recognize differences both among ourselves (young/old, heavy/thin) and between "us" and "them" (American/Japanese, Christian/ Muslim).

But though we think of others as different from us, it is just as true that we are different from them.[21] It is easy to forget that just as we are forming an opinion or registering a judgment about someone who is not part of our particular group, they are doing the same. And because people are individuals as much as they are part of a group, they may not react or behave the way we expect (whether from previous experience with someone from the same group or from an unfounded assumption).

People are by nature "ethnocentric"; that is, we tend to believe that what we live and know is the best and "right" way to live. Based on what we know, we judge and prejudge experiences and situations in order to be able to make decisions. It's called learning. However, many of us do the same thing with people: we apply an experience or generalization to an entire group often without enough or correct information. That is prejudice: treating a subjective assumption about a particular group as objective fact and acting unfairly as a result.[22]

Stereotypes vs. Understanding

"I don't understand you. You don't understand me. What else do we have in common?"

—Ashleigh Brilliant

A stereotype is a label we affix to a person or group based on our own prejudice. It is a generalization, usually distorted or exaggerated, applied to a group that may or may not be based in fact. "Blondes have more fun" is a stereotype. So is "Asians are good at math." There may indeed be individuals who represent those stereotypes but it is both incorrect and unfair to assume the same of *all* blondes or *all* Asians. There is a delicate balance of recognizing and understanding key behavioral or attitudinal characteristics shared by a group of people without making sweeping generalizations.

For example, two Chinese employees in the same office share some similarities, yet both are very different. She may have been brought up in Hong Kong, a commercial city much more connected to Europe and North America than the mainland. He may be more "traditional," having lived in rural mainland China raised during the Cultural Revolution. Both people may display characteristics of both Western and traditional Chinese culture—flexibility and adaptability to new surroundings, a strong work ethic, and deep family ties—and they are both in a new country starting a new life, so they will probably share some of the same challenges. But they are also different, approaching situations and experiences from the perspective of different genders and backgrounds and possibly don't speak the same language.

Both employees probably do, however, encounter the same stereotypes from others who are not Chinese. It is common to hear the remark "All Asians look the same." This is, of course, patently false, but it is interesting to note that I heard the same generalization frequently when I lived in Japan that "All foreigners look the same!" It is an example of how people identify with "Us" versus "Them."

**More than
64%
of Asian Indians
hold a
college degree.**

Another broad stereotype is that Asian Americans are "the model minority": goal-oriented with high levels of education, occupying highly skilled professions and earning high family incomes. Statistically, some Asian Americans do fit this profile. For example, more than 64 percent of Asian Indians hold a college degree (compared to 25 percent of whites). At the same time, however, Southeast Asians have the highest school drop-out rates in the United States.[23]

A further stereotype is "All (fill in the ethnic group) are foreigners". In the above example, one or both of the Chinese employees could easily have been born in New York or Wisconsin. Although more than half of all Asians living in the United States were born elsewhere, many Asian American families have been U.S. citizens for several generations and helped build this country.[24] Of course, this is true of any ethnic or minority group in America. While it is important to recognize that not all people assumed to be foreigners are immigrants, it is equally important to keep in mind that neither does being an immigrant preclude being an American. Immigrants contribute economically, politically and culturally to

American society in the same way native-born Americans do: they go to work or school, raise their children, pay taxes, serve in the military, hold public office, volunteer in the community, and so on.

In her recent study of immigrants working in the fast food industry in New York City, Jennifer Parker Talwar describes stereotypes that different ethnic groups of employees apply to others. The Chinese workers were considered studious and hard-working, but often unwilling to work late because of rigid schedules determined by their families. The Latino employees were thought to be more flexible in their schedules and spontaneous in their interactions because they have a more relaxed home life.[25] Interestingly, Talwar found that these perceptions were reinforced in the work environment by managers because they expected non-Asian employees to be more flexible in their work schedule. Naturally, this translated into tension and ethnic divisions between employees in the restaurants.[26]

To guard against stereotypical thinking, it is important to remember that within every broad ethnic group the characteristics and experiences of people are vastly different. A Cambodian refugee has a completely different history, culture, language and experience from a Taiwanese immigrant, yet both are categorized as Asian American. A Cuban doctor has a completely different set of life experiences than a Mexican rancher, yet both are considered Hispanic or Latino. In her study, Talwar found that managers and workers in several fast-food restaurants made clear social distinctions between themselves within ethnic groups. In one restaurant where most of the staff was Hispanic American, employees divided themselves according to other factors such as age, gender and class. In another restaurant where most of the staff was of Chinese origin, managers made distinctions between the workers based on the region they were from and the dialect they spoke.[27] These divisions created tension and divisions within the workplace, particularly when it came to specific job duties (e.g., those asked to clean the restrooms felt they were being treated as inferior).

Culture Shock

❝ *We see things not as they are, but as we are.* ❞
—*Anais Nin*

True understanding of the pervasiveness of prejudice and stereotypes and the challenges faced by minorities in the United States (or anywhere), is difficult to reach until we have stepped out of our own cultural and geographic comfort zone and plunged ourselves into the sometimes chilly waters of "elsewhere." Experiencing "culture shock" firsthand is a recommended step in overcoming any latent or overt biases about others.

Culture shock can be a motivator or an inhibitor.

Culture shock occurs when we find ourselves in a situation or environment for which we have no point of reference. What we thought we knew about the world, the unwritten rules that guided us along, suddenly no longer apply. We have to re-learn how to live and act, which generally involves learning a new language, forming new relationships, adjusting to a new climate, eating new food, practicing different rules of etiquette, and so on.

Culture shock, like stress, can be a motivator or an inhibitor. Being unable to ask for directions may propel you to learn some language skills quickly because it is in your best interests of survival to be able to communicate. At the same time, regular exclusion from social events because people assume that you "won't fit in" can lead to resentment, discouragement and withdrawal. This can be a result of immersion in a new environment, or a symptom of "reverse culture shock" when a person returns to his or her homeland and discovers that few people can relate to his or her experiences and exposure to life abroad.

When people are separated from their self-identified group—their family, their social network, their familiar work and surroundings—homesickness and a fear of losing or forgetting their identity can also make adapting more difficult. People experiencing culture shock feel isolated, anxious and often helpless. These emotions can result in lower job performance. Obviously, the fewer barriers one encounters in a new environment, particularly in the workplace, the easier it becomes to succeed and contribute productively.

Perhaps, then, to be truly cultured, a person incorporates all of the definitions of the word. A person of culture not only represents a particular group of people with his or her own set of experiences, opinions and behaviors, but also has a sophisticated awareness of those of others and continually cultivates that appreciation as it grows into respect and understanding.

Individual vs. Group Culture

While our culture defines how we see ourselves in relation to others, it also determines how we perceive ourselves within our own "group." American culture is highly individualistic: we reward individual achievement; we root for the underdog; and we strive to be "the best," often at the expense of others. We value independence, competition and personal ambition. We also value equality: most of us believe that all individuals should be treated equally regardless of their status, gender, family role, etc.

Collective cultures, such as Latin American and Asian cultures, are highly group-oriented: more emphasis is placed on a person's position within a collective whole, whether that "whole" is the family, community, work environment or peer group. The feelings and actions of the group heavily influence the feelings and actions of an individual within it. The feelings of others are considered before one's self. Individuals tend to defer to those who hold status, rank or seniority in both professional and personal relationships, and cooperation is the norm. Maintaining harmony and a positive image takes precedence over individual interests and opinions.[28]

In our individualistic culture, we are driven to set and achieve goals, and we prefer to take the most direct path to get the results we want. In group-oriented cultures, the process is the greater concern. How a situation is dealt with is more important than the end result. While we measure success by how closely we meet our objectives, other cultures measure it by how well all of the parties maintain their image or reputation within the group.

An awareness of this difference is necessary for employers and managers to understand attitudes and behavior of employees in the workplace. If a Hispanic American or Asian American employee seems reluctant to "take the lead," the reason may be that he or she is more comfortable participating as part of the wider group rather than wanting to outperform a coworker. He or she may also be reluctant to take a risk that might lead to failure and a negative perception of his or her ability.

It is important to encourage all employees to take risks and reach their full potential for the success of the business. Team-building activities are especially important for connecting people to the group and contribute to a heightened sense of belonging for all staff. When there is a secure and closely-knit team, group-oriented people are less afraid to try new ideas and are more apt to try harder to make the group look good.

Cultural Differences

" ***Understanding is a two-way street.*** *"*
—*Eleanor Roosevelt*

When you are working with a group of people of different nationalities, experiences, opinions and languages, the result can be a productive, creative, competitive team or an unpleasant workplace full of tense, unhappy and uncooperative individuals. Managers who demonstrate an awareness of and respect for cultural differences will motivate their employees to do their best even if the lines of communication are a bit jammed for other reasons.

No one can be expected to fully understand the cultural background of each person in every interaction, and applying generalizations, as discussed earlier, may add another barrier to effective communication. However, if you approach your interactions with every person with an open, accepting and willing-to-learn attitude, you are bound to succeed.

There are several areas to be aware of that often are the source of miscommunication between people of different cultures and that may affect working relationships and productivity. Gestures, posture, eye contact and proximity are all behaviors and communication factors that vary depending on the culture in which you were raised. Other differences to consider include:

- **Social behavior.** Manners and etiquette are quite often a source of confusion and miscommunication among people of different backgrounds. We may be formally taught where the soup spoon goes or how to use chopsticks properly, but completely miss the informal rules that are learned by observation, such as how close to stand next to a person while speaking. Without some understanding of what is appropriate in another culture, it is very easy to give offense without meaning to. One CEO I know made reservations at an upscale steakhouse for a dinner meeting with visiting engineers from India before he realized that they were vegetarians. The guests were gracious and wouldn't hear of changing the venue (or menu) even though their meal options were very limited. Gift-giving is also a tricky area. Giving gifts is perfectly acceptable and expected in some cultures for everything from saying "thank you" to asking for a favor. In the United States, giving expensive or frequent gifts in a business environment may be seen as a bribe and considered illegal as well as unethical.

Americans are schedule-oriented. In other parts of the world, time is more flexible. Workers from other countries may not be as strict about working hours or appointments.

• **Time.** Americans are schedule-oriented. Time is money and the clock rules the day from the second the alarm goes off until it goes off again the next morning. In other parts of the world, such as Latin America and Asia, time is more flexible. Workers from other countries may not be as strict about working hours, appointments or deadlines as their native-born American colleagues, not because they are lazy or indifferent, but because other things may be more important to them.

• **Status.** While some level of social or organizational status is important in most cultures, how it is measured or displayed varies. Respect for seniors is fairly universal, for example, but how people prefer to be addressed is different. It is standard in the United

States to call someone Mr. Smith or Ms. Brown, or address them as Sir or Madam/Ma'am, or more familiarly by their first name. In China, however, it is polite to address people according to their relationship within their family or company organization.[29] Also, Americans tend to display their social status through material possessions such as big homes, well-appointed offices, expensive cars, designer clothing and jewelry. Other cultures are less driven by wealth and assets, and status is revealed through protocol, public seating arrangements or deferential treatment by underlings.

- **Names.** In any culture, one of the easiest ways to show disrespect (or at least disregard) is to get a person's name wrong. It is critical for managers to correctly pronounce and spell their employees' names and to use the preferred form of address. Many Spanish-speaking people have two last names, generally the father's name followed by the mother's name. Married women may have their father's last name followed by their husband's father's last name. For example, if Ana Martínez López marries Javier Hernández Rodríguez, she would become Ana Martínez Rodríguez.[30] In China, the surname comes first. For example, if a man's name is Mr. Wang Jianguo, Wang is the surname. However, "westernized" Chinese may reverse the order to try and assimilate to U.S. custom. If there is any doubt, it is always best to ask. Do not address an employee by a nickname, short form or term of endearment, even if coworkers use more familiar names with each other, unless you are specifically invited to do so.

- **Family.** In the United States, family life often takes a back seat to work responsibilities and many would argue that the breakdown of the traditional American family unit is a result. Extended and immediate family members are often separated by long distance and time spent together is limited to major holidays. Children of single parents and families with two working parents learn to be responsible and independent at a young age, and these traits are considered good training for future work and careers. In other Latin American and Asian cultures, the family is the foundation upon which all else rests. Grandparents, uncles and aunts, siblings, in-laws and children often share the same living space. Children are protected and reared by several authority figures, including but not limited to their parents, and discipline is often strict. Children are expected to obey their elders and not to question authority. Mutual support and obligation is a given: parents look after their children who eventually look after them. This family ethic extends to the workplace as new employees may be unwilling to question their superiors, waiting for guidance to what they are told. At the same time, a closely-knit work team can come to resemble a family for many employees. When this happens, employees will reward you with loyalty and their best efforts.

In group-oriented cultures, the goals and interests of the group take precedence over individual differences and the process of reaching agreement is more important than the final outcome.

• **Conflict.** Differences of opinion or expectation lead to conflict so it is logical to assume that a work environment of diverse opinions and expectations can easily become a hotbed of disagreement and communication breakdown. Again, individual personalities affect how people engage in and react to conflict, but there are cultural tendencies as well. Native-born Americans tend to approach conflict from the perspective of the individual: personal opinions and interests are expressed explicitly to the other party and the expectation is that a satisfactory solution will be reached directly. Issues are confronted openly and closure is reached only when the outcome matches the objective. Other group-oriented cultures, particularly Asian and Latin American, take a different approach: the goals and interests of the group take precedence over individual differences and the process of reaching agreement is more important than the final outcome. It is more important to save face than to score a point (or victory) for your side at the cost of losing face—your own or the other party's.

- **Problem-solving.** American business tends to be a bit of a paradox in that individual initiative and entrepreneurial spirit is applauded, but teamwork and an open exchange of ideas are also highly valued. (Think of all the sports metaphors used in the business world: "We dropped the ball on that one," "We scored a homerun," "That idea came from left field," etc.) We expect debate and discussion and an informed analysis of situations, but in the end, the big decisions are made by one or two people at the top. In China and Japan, it is generally necessary to reach unanimous consensus before decisions are made and carried out. Depending on their cultural background, your employees may or may not expect to play a significant role in solving problems and making decisions.

- **Trust.** Building trust is a key factor in bridging any and all communication and cultural chasms. Employees learn to trust managers who are open, fair and honest. However, honesty may not have the same meaning among different cultures. In the United States, people tend to be straightforward and direct—they tell it like it is (or as they see it). "Beating around the bush" is thought to be a waste of time. In other cultures, a blunt rendering of the "truth" may not be considered desirable or appropriate, especially if it is unpleasant or involves upsetting someone else or losing face. It is important for supervisors to communicate to employees that it is okay to make mistakes and learn, and encourage staff to be forthright about issues that concern them.

CHAPTER 4

Effective Communication

> **Nothing in life is more important than the ability to communicate effectively.**
>
> —Gerald Ford

Communication

Communication is the process of sending, receiving and interpreting messages. We use all of our available sensory organs to formulate and make sense of these messages: mouth and tongue to speak; ears to listen; eyes to watch; hands to write, draw, gesture or feel vibrations; and our brains to translate all of the linguistic codes and non-verbal signals into thoughts and words. Communication involves spoken and written language, body language and posture, facial expressions, and tone of voice. Considering that the world's six billion people speak over 6,000 distinct languages, the combinations of these elements together make up an infinite number of possible messages and meanings.

As human beings, we communicate with each other for a myriad of reasons: to express our thoughts and emotions, to give and request information, to persuade or debate ideas, to understand and interact with other human beings, to argue or resolve conflict. Sometimes communication is intentional, sometimes it is not. Successful communication only occurs when the message we intend to send is the same one that is received.

Successful communication only occurs when the message we intend to send is the same one that is received.

In order to communicate, we are guided by different sets of "rules." There are general rules that determine our cultural behavior (e.g., Americans smile and nod when they greet each other; Japanese bow at the waist) and more specific rules among particular groups within a culture, such as within the military or a college sorority. Then there are rules that are unique to particular relationships—we may shake hands with a new acquaintance but hug an old friend.

Over time and through experience, we learn the rules of communication that are relevant to our lives. For example, toddlers eventually learn that temper tantrums are inappropriate means of communicating and begin to express themselves through words rather than screams. They learn to be more effective at getting their message understood and their needs fulfilled in ways that are acceptable to others in their cultural surroundings.

As adults, when we find ourselves immersed in another culture with a totally different set of behavioral rules and language, we have to learn to communicate effectively all over again. Our goals of communicating in our new environment go beyond wanting to be fed and managing other daily survival issues. They include learning something new, developing new relationships, building trust, understanding different points of view, and working with others toward a common goal.

Words and actions mean different things to different people, even among those with a common language and culture (e.g., people who do not share the same sense of humor). We can communicate a message to someone that we are angry by walking into a room frowning, when in fact we are trying to remember where we put the car keys. Because the messages we send are made up of our own perceptions and assumptions (our culture) and the fact that we are not always completely aware of those messages, effective communication is highly complex and ambiguous.

Non-Verbal Communication

" To know what people really think, pay regard to what they do, rather than what they say. "
—René Descartes

According to some researchers, words make up only 10 percent of the actual message in face-to-face communication; the rest of the message is conveyed non-verbally through body language (50 percent) and tone of voice (40 percent).[31] Considering how much our culture dictates our physical behavior, gestures, etc., the fact that communication depends so heavily on our non-verbal expression emphasizes how easily miscommunication can occur with someone from another culture. When there is a significant difference between the sender's culture and the receiver's culture, there is a greater chance of misunderstanding.[32]

Types of non-verbal cues include:

- **Spatial cues:** distance between speakers, seating arrangements.

- **Visual cues:** facial expressions, eye contact, body movements, clothing.

- **Vocal cues:** tone, volume, hesitation, speed of speech, articulation.

Every person has a unique style of communicating that may or may not reflect the "norms" of his or her culture. Thinking about our own non-verbal behavior and being aware of others' decreases the chance of being misinterpreted, but does not guarantee that misunderstandings will disappear.

North Americans wave their hand up and down to signify "good-bye"; Japanese make the same gesture to indicate "come here."

Most of the rules of non-verbal communication in any culture are unwritten. Unlike grammar and vocabulary that you can study in a book or practice in a language class, non-verbal rules are best learned by observation, imitation and feedback. Even if someone is fluent in another language, it is difficult to understand and master what specific gestures mean in another culture especially when the gesture looks similar to one we use in our culture. For example, North Americans wave their hand up and down to signify "good-bye"; Japanese make the same gesture to indicate "come here."

In a recent radio interview, a Canadian expert in intercultural relations related an anecdote about misinterpreted non-verbal communication. Several lawyers visiting from South Africa were chatting in a hotel elevator as the door opened on another group of professionals who had been talking in the hallway. As the second group entered the elevator, they stopped talking, turned to face forward and waited quietly until they reached their floor. The South African visitors interpreted this behavior as insulting and racist, not realizing that most Canadians behave that way in any elevator no matter who is riding in it. (It is generally considered respectful of other people sharing a small space to not inflict your conversation on them; looking at them directly is also considered rude or possibly even threatening.[33])

Body language sends messages in ways we may not think about. Touching someone on the arm while speaking may be natural to one person but an affront, or sexual invitation, to someone else. Posture, habits of dress and facial expressions are all capable of communicating an array of conflicting messages that may or may not be intended:

- Respect/Disrespect
- Interest/Boredom
- Agreement/Disagreement
- Emotion/Disinterest
- Flexibility/Rigidity

It is common for North Americans to lean against a wall with their hands in their pockets when chatting with a friend or colleague. To many Asians, this posture is considered rude and lazy. In our culture, we value direct eye contact as an indicator of confidence and honesty; in many parts of the world, looking someone directly in the eye when speaking is seen as disrespectful and aggressive. In the United States, people generally maintain a five-foot "zone" between them during a conversation—any closer and we complain the other person is "invading our space." Someone from a Latin American country would move in considerably closer to talk, while a Japanese person would find five feet uncomfortably close.

In China, where negative responses are considered rude, silence often signals disagreement.

Asian culture is "high context"; that is, people use non-verbal cues (gestures, tone) and environmental settings (such as seating arrangements) to dictate messages and behavior. North American culture is "low context" in that we rely heavily on verbal language to convey messages.[34] While social relationships and business "understandings" are emphasized in China, for example, American business is much more dependent upon signed contracts. Saying "no" in the United States is fairly straightforward, but in China, where negative responses are considered rude, silence often signals disagreement. Whereas we find "awkward silences" very uncomfortable, the Chinese consider no response to be less awkward than direct refusal.[35]

Another important aspect of communication is one that involves behavior and may be exercised verbally and non-verbally. The concept of "face" is extremely important to many cultures, particularly Asian and Latin American. "Saving face" refers to the cultural imperative of maintaining your reputation and status in the eyes of other people. It is possible to "give face" whereby you make someone look good by virtue of a compliment or endorsement. Conversely, "losing face" occurs when others perceive you to have lost respect, either due to your own behavior or by insult from someone else. In the United States, getting fired is difficult, but people generally understand that there are often reasons for termination that are not reflective of the ability of the worker (economic downturn that leads to layoffs or reorganization of company structure). However, in some cultures, such as China, getting fired is a huge loss of face as it is seen as being professionally inadequate.[36]

Face includes many features including pride, honor, shame, trust, disgrace, dignity, insult, prestige, commitment, reliability and professionalism. If any of these values are compromised, an individual will be felt or seen to have lost face. For example, arriving late for a meeting or not showing at all can cause both parties to lose face; doing so indicates you do not accord the waiting party appropriate respect or consideration and that you yourself are not particularly conscientious.

While it is impossible to learn and correctly interpret every individual's style of non-verbal communication, it is possible to apply some general practices to limit potential misunderstandings.

- **Be self-aware.** Try to be aware of the messages you are sending to others. Watch how people react to you and ask for direct feedback. You may be surprised at what your body language communicates (or doesn't) to others.

- **Look for patterns.** Get to know the non-verbal habits of people you work or interact with regularly. Are they the same for different situations? Someone who clears his throat constantly may have a "behavioral tic" when you thought he was interjecting or disagreeing in a meeting.

- **Clarify.** If you are unsure about a person's non-verbal message, ask for an explanation. Does a raised eyebrow indicate skepticism about your idea, or is it a sign of concentration? Someone from a different culture may use a gesture that has a completely different meaning in the United States. Don't assume it means what you think.

- **Don't imitate.** If you don't know for certain what a gesture means in another language or culture, don't use it.

- **Be aware of gender differences.** Even within cultures, female body language can be different from males. For example, in Japan, women often cover their mouths when they laugh and eat. Men tend not to. Similarly there are "male" and "female" techniques for using chopsticks. In the United States, men tend to cross their legs with one ankle over the opposite knee; women cross their legs with their thighs closed.

The Power of Language

" Language, as a symbol, determines much of the nature and quality of our experience. "
—Sonia Johnson

Most of us rely on oral and written language to learn about and interact with the rest of the world. (Note: While American Sign Language [ASL], Signed English and other signed communication methods used by people experiencing deafness and speech challenges are valid and respected languages, they are more accurately defined as non-verbal as they use gestures to indicate words, punctuation and numbers.) While there are thousands of different dialects around the globe, about half of the total world population speaks one of ten languages: Mandarin Chinese, Hindi, Spanish, English, Bengali, Arabic, Russian, Portuguese, Japanese and German.[37]

Every language is comprised of words which are symbols that represent concepts and ideas. Whatever language we first learn to speak reflects the perceptions and experiences of the people with whom we share a common background. Language and culture are interconnected in a chicken-and-egg kind of way: culture determines the concepts for which words are created and the evolution of that language, in turn, influences the culture and how we think. There are words for flora and fauna in the languages of nations where those species exist that cannot be translated into other languages. (Or, think of the example of dozens of words the Inuit have created to describe snow.) But also, language evolves to reflect rapid technological and cultural change. Twenty years ago the words "e-mail," "laptop" and "cell phone" did not exist in English or any other language.

Words alone are important tools in building effective communication, but they can rarely get the job done by themselves. We depend on context and non-verbal cues to give us the meaning of words. For the 2,000 or so words we use every day to read a newspaper and converse fluently, there are tens of thousands of dictionary definitions, and those are changing all the time.[38] To communicate, we rely on our understanding of the words themselves, how they are spoken, where, when and by whom. We match them to the ideas and experiences in our brains and interpret them according to what we already know or think or feel.

When given contextual meaning, language is power. The childhood chant "Sticks and stones can break my bones but names will never hurt me" encourages children to ignore name-calling. But anyone who has ever been subjected to it will attest that names do hurt. The words we choose to describe a person (or group) reflect our own thoughts and perceptions about him or her, but how they are used can influence how the receiver feels about himself or herself.

It used to be perfectly acceptable in our culture to label visible minorities, or anyone "different" from the majority population (e.g., White Christian), with terms that were derogatory because they were intended to convey inferiority, disrespect, fear and hate. Since the civil rights and feminism movements of the 1960s and 70s when the traditional economic and political power structure was forced to recognize a change in social values and thinking, that language came to be considered inappropriate in our culture and we created laws to eliminate (or at least discourage) its usage. Our thinking influenced our language, which influenced our thinking some more.

Today, rather than a minority of open-minded liberal radicals, the majority of decent people in our society are offended by negative remarks targeted at any group. "Political correctness" has been internalized over time so that our youth automatically accept diversity—in their homes, in the classroom, on the playground, in the mall, in the workplace—as a given. Their acceptance is natural rather than legislated.

In the business world, however, not everyone is so enlightened, as the millions of dollars spent on lawsuits would attest. A wise employer would take care to monitor the kind of language that is used and tolerated in the workplace.

The Written Word

" When written in Chinese, the word 'crisis' is composed of two characters— one represents danger, and the other represents opportunity. "
—*Saul David Alinsky*

The jury is still out on whether or not it is easier to learn to write a language or to speak it. Obviously, we learn to speak our mother tongue long before we are taught to hold a pencil and form words on paper. But learning a second language is another process.

Public school students in Japan are taught English throughout their school career, but very few of the several hundred that I taught could speak a sentence. Their writing skills, however, were quite advanced. At the end of high school, most students have had ten or more years of English grammar instruction, almost all of which was taught in Japanese by Japanese teachers of English. Immigrants to the United States may or may not have had a similar experience in their native school systems.

While oral English skills are likely the most important for foreign-born employees to develop, especially if they are working in the service industry, written communication skills are also necessary for job performance. Employees are required not only to receive written information—forms, schedules, safety rules and regulations, policy handbooks, maintenance manuals, memos, maps, client contact information, etc.—but also to send it (receipts for customers, promotional material, completed task checklists, menus, inventory lists, and so on).

Few business environments are without computers these days. On the one hand, technology can break down communication problems: learning a few key strokes to operate machinery or a cash register can be easily accomplished by anyone in any language. However, the Internet and e-mail are an entrenched part of most people's work day, whether "the office" is a restaurant, a taxi cab company, a call center or hotel, and English is still the main language of operations. Regardless of whether the words are on a computer screen or a piece of paper, comprehension of written English is critical to the completion of many job tasks.

Companies with the resources to draft internal communication in the language(s) spoken and read by employees would benefit, as would those who are able to have English-language documents translated. Obviously, the likelihood of misunderstandings would be sharply decreased. However, if producing written materials in second or third languages is not an immediate option, the following considerations should be kept in mind to ensure that messages are received:

- Make the purpose of the information immediately clear. Use a subject line to get attention.

- Use short and specific words and sentences. Don't write, "During the course of the week, we've received several calls"; instead write, "This week we received 12 calls."

- Use short paragraphs (5 to 10 lines) that address one topic at a time.

- If there is a lot of information, use numbers or point form to highlight important points.

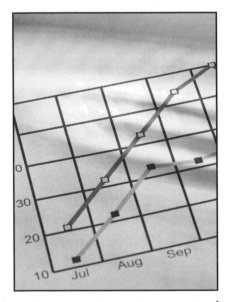

- Avoid slang, jargon or acronyms unless they are explicitly defined.

- Use pictures, charts and graphs to illustrate your point whenever possible.

- Consider attaching important information to paychecks to be sure everyone receives it. Follow up with employees to check for understanding.

Use pictures, charts and graphs to illustrate your point whenever possible.

Communication Styles

" The most important thing in communication is to hear what isn't being said. "
—Peter Drucker

Researchers of communication styles study human thinking processes to learn how we use language to determine our behavior. One theory, called Neuro-Linguistic Programming (NLP), is a communication model conceived by John Grinder and Richard Bandler to enhance effective communication. NLP studies how we organize information gathered by our senses and language to "program" how to act. It suggests that we organize what we know into mental maps determined by three primary methods of perceiving the world:

1. **Visual.** Visual communicators—about 35 percent of people—think by picturing things in their minds. Their perceptions and understanding come mainly from what they see. For this group, appearance plays an important role in sending and receiving messages.

2. **Auditory.** Auditory communicators—25 percent of people—make sense of information by analyzing sounds. How things are said convey more meaning than what is said.

3. **Kinesthetic.** Kinesthetic communicators—the majority at 40 percent—get more information from touching and feeling. Instinct and emotion guide their responses and actions.[39]

While NLP has its detractors and skeptics[40]—it has a reputation for being an alternative psychology—it is useful to consider the possibility that different people perceive and process language and information

Visual
communicators—35%

Auditory
communicators—25%

Kinesthetic
communicators—40%

Present important information three ways: orally, visually and kinesthetically.

in different ways. Some people I know remember information by singing it; when I hear words, I picture them (and spell them) simultaneously in my head. From the perspective of someone communicating in English as a second or third language, understanding how he or she might be applying the codes and cues to form meaning is an important step in enhancing comprehension.

In a work environment where employees' English comprehension is limited, an English-speaking manager wanting to give instructions or important information might think about communicating the message visually, aurally and concretely. Ways to do this might include:

- Listing highlights in point form on a transparency, displayed on an overhead projector and reviewed orally in more detail, and photocopies of the list distributed to everyone.

- Frequently repeating and summarizing important points.

- Covering small amounts of information (or one topic at a time) in a single workshop or meeting.

- Playing a short video to illustrate specific information (e.g., on workplace safety) with accompanying booklets either distributed or displayed in a central area for later reference.

- Circulating memos by e-mail and posting easy-to-read hard copies in a central, accessible area (and face-to-face follow-up with individuals to ensure understanding).

- Illustrating numbers and figures with graphs and charts.

- Using international symbols that can be understood in different cultures and languages (e.g., red circle with diagonal line to indicate "prohibited").

- Using props to reinforce information or instructions (e.g., if you want to explain how a new uniform is to be worn, wear it or have it in your hand).

- Demonstrating the correct way to complete tasks and use equipment.

- Communication styles are as varied as individuals. While there is a generalization that Americans and Latin Americans tend to be forthright and direct while Asians tend to be less so, there are obviously gradations in between. If someone is shy, his or her communication style will not be the same as someone who is outgoing and animated regardless of cultural background. Personalities play a large role in determining effective communication within the workplace. If you are a manager who is not a gregarious "people person," it will be somewhat more challenging for you to manage employees who are. Similarly, if you are an A-type personality—energetic, driven, organized—it will be more difficult to relate to employees who prefer to keep to themselves and do their work autonomously.

Although everyone uses different styles of communication depending on the situation, our physical and mental states and to whom we are speaking, most of us have a predominant style that is shaped by all of the factors that make us individuals: personality, age, gender, religion, education, physical ability, and so on. Our overall communication style influences how we send and receive messages. One theory divides communication styles into three categories:

- Passive communicators put the thoughts and feelings of others before their own. They are often overly apologetic, have stooped posture, avoid eye contact and convey poor self-esteem. They usually doubt their ability and fear negative feedback.

- Assertive communicators acknowledge the thoughts and feelings of others but maintain their own. They are direct and relaxed, and project both confidence and respect for others. They take responsibility for their opinions and actions and are open and easy to talk to.

- Aggressive communicators have little regard for others' thoughts and feelings. They are loud and tense, and convey anger, fear and disrespect. They tend to be easily frustrated and quick to enter into conflict.[41]

To engage and encourage "passive" employees (and calm or deflect "aggressive" ones), a manager might consider the following actions:

- Carefully moderate staff meetings. Institute a one-at-a-time speaker rule. Ask quiet or reluctant employees for their thoughts. Encourage people to speak to you after the meeting if they are uncomfortable in a group setting.

- Have a written agenda for everyone to follow. If there are other issues that arise, list them on paper or a white board and discuss them in turn. If time is limited, table them for discussion at another meeting in the immediate future. Let people know their concerns are heard and will be addressed.

- Keep your voice at normal, audible levels. Speak clearly and vary your inflection (don't drone on in a monotone or be excessively loud and animated).

- Walk around the room, if possible. Don't hover over anyone, but shortening physical distance can engage your audience and stimulate them to pay closer attention than if you are seated at the end of a conference room or cafeteria table.

- Listen to each person's input. Don't interrupt unless the speaker is veering off topic, monopolizing the meeting or getting agitated.

- If you must interrupt, do so respectfully. "Excuse me (name), your comments are appreciated but we are close to the clock and need to cover a few other things. Can we pursue your thoughts on this issue a bit later (after the meeting, at lunch, etc.)?"

- If you have a volatile employee(s), post meeting rules or office expectations. (Example: Everyone is heard. Personal attacks are unacceptable. Foul language is inappropriate. All opinions are valid.)

- Encourage teamwork and cooperation by highlighting your company mission statement with a banner in the staffroom. (Example: Our mission is to offer the highest quality of product/ service in the region/industry with a skilled team of committed and valued employees.)

- Make a point of thanking people for their input; show genuine appreciation for participating and taking initiative.

Communication Barriers

" *What we've got here is a failure to communicate.* "
—*Frank R. Pierson*

In an ideal world, assertiveness would be the standard—people would express their rights and needs with confidence, would listen and respond to others with empathy, and everyone would communicate clearly and easily. Obviously this is not the case and many barriers can affect good communication.

Communication breaks down when messages are not received or they are received in a way that was not intended by the sender. Emotion can be a significant barrier to communication: someone who is angry is unlikely to be open to a give-and-take exchange. Fear is another stumbling block. People who are afraid of hurting feelings or of receiving a negative reaction may not express themselves at all or may communicate a message that is not what they really mean. For example, an employee might fail to ask for direction in completing a job task he or she doesn't understand for fear the boss or co-worker will think they he or she is incompetent. Similarly, when asked how things are progressing, he or she might smile and say, "Okay." or "Great." when the actual message is "Help!"

Some communication experts believe that in any language and culture, people use speech for four main purposes:

1. Asking others to do things.

2. Promising or refusing to do things.

3. Determining whether something is true or false.

4. Declaring an objective or stating something new.[42]

In his workbook, *Working Together: Succeeding in a Multicultural Organization*, Dr. George Simons suggests asking yourself the following four questions after every meeting with a person from another culture:

1. Did I ask something of the other person or they of me?

2. Did I promise something to them or they to me?

3. What did we tell each other about what is true or false?

4. Did either of us commit ourselves to a new attitude, direction, definition or state of affairs?

Simons suggests that if you can answer all of those questions after a business transaction, you will know that understanding has taken place and agreement has been reached. For example:

Manager: *Luis, can you meet me in my office in ten minutes and bring your pay stub?*

Luis: *Yes, I'll be there at 9:30. Is there something wrong?*

Manager: *There was a problem with deductions last week.*

Luis: *I thought my check looked less than usual.*

Manager: *I apologize for that. I'd like to explain where the mistake was made.*

In this exchange, the manager has asked for a meeting and the employee has promised to attend. The manager has indicated that something is true and has stated his objective for the meeting. Both parties understand what has happened and what will happen next. Had the manager simply asked the employee to meet him in his office without explaining further, the employee may have worried there was bad news in store, misunderstanding the message due to lack of information.

Other obstacles to effective communication include:

- **Boredom.** If the receiver is not interested in the subject because it is not relevant to his or her experience or is difficult to grasp, he or she will tune out and miss the message. Example: A computer programmer starts talking at length to a non-technical co-worker about the problems in the latest application of a software utility. After a few minutes, the co-worker is probably thinking about lunch. The programmer feels snubbed and insulted; the co-worker is impatient and may feel guilty for not listening.

Boredom, distractions, time constraints and negativity are all communication obstacles.

- **Distractions.** If a person is preoccupied by problems or tasks unrelated to the immediate conversation, it is difficult to concentrate on listening and responding appropriately. Example: An employee is distracted and distant in a staff meeting because his or her parent is in the hospital undergoing surgery. The meeting leader is frustrated by a seeming lack of interest and participation; the employee is stressed and worried and has missed important information. Also, physical distractions such as noise, clutter and lack of space can interfere with sending and receiving clear messages.

- **Time.** Deadlines, meetings, work schedules and appointments all limit the amount of time available in any exchange of information. Example: You have a meeting with a client at 9:15 and your employee wants to discuss a raise. There may not be sufficient time to fully discuss the issue so both parties may miss information critical to the decision-making process. Also, if you are watching the clock, you are more than likely thinking about what is coming next, not listening to what is being said now.

- **Negativity.** When a person feels negative or disapproving about a subject (or the person talking about it), he or she tends to be close-minded. Instead of listening and acknowledging what the other person is saying, he or she is formulating an argument or opinion against it. The response is viewed as uncooperative or confrontational and provokes a similar response in the other person. Example: Your employee is late for the third morning in a row and you begin your reprimand when he or she comes into your office before he or she has a chance to explain that the baby has chicken pox and has been up through the night all week. You are hostile and your employee is defensive.

- **Assumptions.** Sometimes we base our decisions on previous experience or opinions without considering all the facts. When we jump to conclusions without looking at new information, we miss messages and opportunities. Example: A prospective employee walks into your office for an interview with a pierced eyebrow, nostril and nose. You have an aversion to this style of adornment and make up your mind that he or she will not do a good job even before the interview has started. You don't bother to read the resumé that describes excellent qualifications and references. You have made an unfair assessment and the job-seeker feels devalued.

- **Language.** Although it is the primary tool in communication, language can also be one of the biggest barriers. People who speak the same language can easily misunderstand vocabulary, slang, idioms, regional accents and pronunciation. Australians, Britons and Americans all speak English, but many expressions common to each nationality (and to people from different regions within those nations) are unintelligible to others. Example: An Australian friend delivered a presentation on his company's latest automation product to a group of oil industry executives. At the end, one of the executives said, "Well, that was impressive." The Australian replied enthusiastically, "Ah, Mate, it's Mickey Mouse!" (In Australia, "Mickey Mouse" means wonderful, but the Americans at the table thought he meant it was unimportant or of little value.) Because of two words with different meanings in the same language, the sale was nearly lost.

When people speak among themselves in a different language, others around them may feel excluded or talked about.

When you add foreign languages and cultures to the mix, the number of barriers increases. Occasionally people shut down as soon as they see you and fail to recognize that you have just spoken to them in their native language. The brain tells them that this person speaking doesn't look like they should be able to communicate with them, so their ears turn off and a perfectly clear and meaningful message is not received. (This happens to tourists all the time even when they are fluent in the language of the country they are visiting.)

Also, many people assume that if someone has a poor command of the language being spoken, then that person lacks intelligence or has a hearing problem. This common misconception explains the disturbing phenomenon of people raising their voices and speak-ing ver-y slow-ly to another person for whom English is not their first language.

Finally, within the diverse workplace, language can be the source of tension among employees. When people speak among themselves in a different language, others around them may feel excluded or talked about—paranoia and resentment becomes the norm. Managers are faced with the challenge of finding a way to balance the interests of individuals as well as the company so that people can maintain a comfort level by speaking their native language without alienating their co-workers or interfering with productivity. Restricting employees to speaking only English at work is considered to be discriminatory under the federal EEOC regulations unless such a restriction is proven to be a valid business necessity.

Other options to consider in lowering the language barrier include:

- Take classes in the language of the employees you supervise.

- Provide support to employees with limited English skills. If the company cannot offer ESL classes in-house, direct employees to community resources and classes. Pay for instruction if at all possible.

- Offer opportunities for English-speaking employees to learn the "other" language(s) spoken by co-workers either during working hours, or at lunch or after work (e.g., a weekly gathering over a meal). Invite employees to act as tutors or workshop leaders, or hire a local resource to conduct formal or informal classes.

- Encourage bilingual employees to act as "buddy" translators to facilitate communication when necessary, but do not put repeated onus on any one person (unless they have been hired specifically for the purpose of translating).

- Translate important documents and information (e.g., health and safety instructions) into as many languages as needed. All employees should be able to understand information pertinent to their jobs.

- Offer opportunities—through formal cultural sensitivity training or informal colleague forums—for people to understand each other's positions. Co-workers are likely to be speaking Mandarin or Spanish to each other because it is the most efficient way to convey work-related information, not because they are being rude or because they are not motivated to learn to speak English.

- It is not realistic to expect that communication will always flow smoothly and that messages will always be sent and received as they were intended, but neither is it productive to assume that barriers will always get in the way of understanding. The key to minimizing miscommunication is an awareness of the possible pitfalls and a willingness to work at finding ways around them.

CHAPTER 5

The Workplace

> **"The art of communication is the language of leadership."**
> —James Humes

Effective Management

To successfully operate a business made up of people with diverse backgrounds, effective managers are willing and able to build a team that brings together different points of view to meet a common goal or goals, such as higher profits, better customer service, cooperation and understanding, etc. They foster an environment where every person is able to contribute to their full potential. It takes time—sometimes a long time—to change attitudes and ensure true collaboration takes place, among employees and between employees and management. Some of the critical elements that allow that collaboration are awareness, openness, empathy and leadership.

- **Awareness.** Effective managers and employers recognize when and where the barriers to communication and success exist. They learn about other cultural values to understand better how to bridge the gap by asking questions and observing behavior. They are aware of their own assumptions about people from other cultures, and the fact that their own cultural norms may not apply to their employees. The one correct assumption they do make is that theirs is not the only way to communicate.

- **Openness.** Effective managers are willing to try different approaches to communicating and are willing to practice them until they are comfortable and successful at conveying—and receiving—real messages. They look for and encourage ways to make communication work rather than blame the other party for the failure.

- **Empathy.** Effective managers acknowledge the feelings and interests of their employees by actively listening to their message and responding in a genuine and appropriate way. They suspend judgment about the person and evaluate the issue according to how it affects the individual's and the company's success.

- **Leadership.** Good business leaders and managers have a vision of where the company is, where it should be and how to get it there. They share that vision by open communication and personal example to motivate and inspire employees to follow. But it doesn't happen automatically; it takes trust, commitment and time to exercise the qualities of a good leader. A good leader:

  - Implements a team approach, facilitating cooperation and group decision-making.

- Demonstrates company standards of high performance.

- Gives direction without micromanaging.

- Delegates authority and trusts the ability of team members.

- Encourages individual strengths of employees (especially when they lack those strengths themselves).

- Treats everyone fairly but not necessarily the same way (responds to individual needs).

- Supports team by offering advice or help when requested (acts as a coach).

- Evaluates problems and performance objectively and constructively.

- Listens with understanding and open to creative problem-solving.

Listening

"Courage is what it takes to stand up and speak; courage is also what it takes to sit down and listen."
—*Winston Churchill*

Contrary to popular belief, the passive act of hearing is not the same as "listening." Listening is an active, purposeful skill, learned with practice, which is critical to successful communication. When we are listening to gather information—paying attention, thinking about the information, drawing conclusions and filing it away for later recall—we are listening "deliberatively." Our school system teaches us to do this to retain information, analyze it and form opinions about it. In two-way communication, however, the goal is to understand the information as well as the person imparting it, which is a more empathic process.[43]

Listening is an active, purposeful skill, learned with practice, which is critical to successful communication.

Active listening requires focusing attention on what is said as well as what is not said: the words are interpreted in context with the tone of voice, posture, gestures, facial expression, emphasis on particular words, choice of vocabulary, hesitations and volume. Only by really listening to all of these cues is the listener is able to identify with the speaker, synthesize the meaning and respond appropriately.

It is especially important for managers of employees who do not speak English, or speak it well, to know how to actively listen. Effective managers exercise active listening skills to allow greater understanding of problems, promote open relationships with employees, build trust and credibility and inspire loyalty and performance. When employees feel that they are genuinely heard and understood, they are much more likely to "go the extra mile" in their jobs.

It is difficult to break habits that prevent us from listening effectively. It takes a conscious effort to concentrate on meaning when the message is difficult or hard to follow. It is easy to "tune out" when we are bombarded by noise or a droning voice or a boring subject. Conversely, we can let our emotions get in the way of active listening:

a particular word, or our opinion about the person speaking, might trigger a feeling that colors the way that we interpret everything else that is said. Some of the other things we often do that interfere with active listening include:

- **Filtering:** hearing only what we want to hear and blocking or ignoring new information or information that is contrary to our expectations.

- **Anticipating:** thinking or "knowing" what the other person is going to say next and missing what they are actually saying.

- **Rehearsing:** planning what we are going to say next instead of listening.

- **Deflecting:** changing the subject because we are not interested or wish to avoid conflict.

To avoid these pitfalls, there are specific behaviors that facilitate more effective listening:

- **Look at the person who is speaking.** Make an effort to tune out background noise and minimize distractions and tune in to the verbal and non-verbal messages being given.

- **Step into the speaker's shoes.** Try to imagine yourself as the speaker—would you be nervous speaking to you? How would you want to feel? What can you do as the listener to make the speaker feel at ease and heard? (Stop typing that e-mail; turn off the cell phone; close the door.)

- **Don't interrupt the speaker.** If you don't understand something, wait for a pause and ask for clarification, or ask the person to repeat what they said.

- **Rephrase what you've heard.** In your own words, tell the person what you understand them to mean.

- **Be patient.** A non-native English speaker might pause frequently searching for the right words; respectfully give them time to say what they mean. Offer help if the person is struggling.

- **Watch the speaker's response to you.** We often change our message to reflect how our audience is responding. Did the speaker suddenly change their tone or words because you unconsciously crossed your arms or took a step backwards? Be aware of your own body language.

- **Find a reason for listening.** If you know that you do not enjoy listening to the person or the subject, try to find the payoff to do it anyway. Maybe you will learn something of value to you personally, or paying attention to this issue now will avoid having to spend time doing it later when you feel even less like listening! At the very least, the payoff to the company will be that this person will feel valued and heard and will likely respond by doing his or her job better.

Effective listening produces immediate results in communication.

Effective listening produces immediate results in communication. The person speaking feels understood and validated and the person listening receives a more meaningful message. This promotes further open communication, greater understanding and better working relationships. An obvious but critical component of listening is demonstrating our understanding, or lack of it, to the speaker in the form of feedback.

Feedback

> *" You can tell whether a man is clever by his answers.*
> *You can tell whether a man is wise by his questions. "*
>
> —Naguib Mahfouz

Feedback is the reaction we have to information as it is processed in our brains that indicates not only that we have heard the message, but that we are participating in the communication process. It involves monitoring the effect of our message on the other person, evaluating why the listener reacts a particular way, and adjusting our next message to reflect that the listener has an impact on the communication.[44] Feedback occurs when both the speaker and the listener affect each other during communication. (If there was no response from one party, the other would soon stop talking and find someone else more receptive to two-way communication.)

Giving feedback reinforces that the message conveyed has been received and understood, or indicates that it hasn't. It can be verbal or non-verbal. When a listener nods or interjects, "Yes, I see." during a conversation, he or she is giving feedback that says, "I am listening." or "I agree with you." At the same time, a listener saying nothing with a puzzled frown is giving feedback that "I don't understand." or "I do not agree."

Receiving feedback is how we gauge how effectively we have conveyed our message. Being able to "read" the listener's reaction allows us to know whether or not they understood our meaning, but also enables us to modify our own behavior and improve our ways of communicating. For example, if I start to describe my five-year-old's playground antics to a co-worker who does not enjoy children, I am likely to receive feedback that tells me that he is being polite but is not really interested, he is busy with something else, or I am talking

Asking questions can be a highly effective form of feedback.

too much. I, in turn, can change the subject or take the hint and go away.

Generally, the more feedback is given and received in any exchange, the more accurate the message and understanding will be. That is, of course, provided the feedback doesn't shut the other person down. If your response to the message is critical or judgmental, the speaker is likely to get defensive and less likely to engage in further conversation. Negative feedback is generally destructive, focusing on what the person said or did wrong. It is usually blaming, confrontational and does not contribute to open dialogue or improvement.

Asking questions, however, can be a highly effective form of feedback. Finding out as much as possible from the speaker by asking open-ended questions that require more than a yes or no response indicates to the speaker that you are interested and engaged in what they are saying. It is important to phrase questions in a way that is not threatening or accusing. For example, if an employee comes to you with a job-related difficulty, instead of asking, "Why did you do that?" try "How did you go about that?" or "What are your ideas on how to improve this situation?"

Paraphrasing is another effective way of giving feedback. As in active listening, restating what you have heard allows you to clarify the issue with the speaker and indicate that you are trying to understand. It also summarizes the conversation to focus on the main points, which may make the problem-solving process (if necessary) easier.

Effective managers can improve their communication skills by practicing the following feedback behaviors:

- **Don't interrupt.** As in active listening, waiting for the speaker to finish is an important part of the give-and-take of communicating. It is difficult to do—interrupting is a bad habit that most of us engage in as a normal part of animated conversation.

- **Paraphrase.** Summarize what you have heard and ask if your understanding is correct before offering a comment.

- **Suspend judgment.** Avoid analyzing and evaluating the person or the problem. Although it is at times appropriate and necessary to give opinions and advice, generally managers and employers are not psychiatrists or counselors. Appropriate feedback encourages the speaker to self-evaluate and draw his or her own conclusions.

- **Be constructive.** If the communication is focused on evaluating employee performance, acknowledge where things are going well and suggest practical and achievable solutions to existing problems. Constructive feedback leaves an employee feeling helped rather than attacked. It fosters cooperation and motivates employees to meet personal and company goals and improve skills.

- **Be aware of your verbal and non-verbal responses.** If your words do not match your body language and behavior, the feedback you give will likely be received as false or confusing. Similarly, if you constantly nod or smile, you will probably not be perceived as sincere. Feedback should be genuine and specific to the message.

Training

" *A goal properly set is halfway reached.* **"**
—*Abraham Lincoln*

In order for any employee to succeed personally and contribute positively to the company, he or she needs to know what to do and why it needs to be done. Managers and employers need to be able to communicate the skills and tasks required for the job and how to perform them for optimum benefit to the business. Employees need to be appropriately trained in these tasks. They also need to have clear objectives and goals as well as an understanding of the reasons behind them. Managers need to "connect the dots" for new hires, especially if language is an issue. To use a familiar sports metaphor, every player on the team has a position. Each player needs to know what their position is, how to play it, and how important his or her contribution is for the team to function well and win the game.

Employees need to be appropriately trained and have clear objectives.

The most obvious place to start is to give employees a formal job description, written and explained orally in detail. Because authority is so highly valued by many Hispanic American and Asian American workers, it is a good idea to explicitly state the chain of command—who is to report to whom and when. If there is a problem with payroll, who is the best person to talk to? It is also important to explain (with all employees) how to prioritize the tasks in their job. Is it more important to talk to a customer in the lobby or answer the phone?

Small-business owners and managers may or may not be directly involved in the training of their staff, depending on the size of the company and the work involved. However, in his book *Developing the Leaders Around You,* John Maxwell outlines a five-step training process that is useful for managers or trainers to follow in any work environment, especially where there are communication and/or culture issues such as a deep aversion to taking risks and the fear of failure in front of others:

1. **Model.** Perform the task with the trainee watching. Explain each step from the beginning.

2. **Mentor.** Perform the task again with the trainee assisting. Explain why as well as how to complete each step.

3. **Monitor.** Have the trainee complete the task while you watch, assisting and correcting when necessary. Ask the trainee to explain the steps to you to reinforce understanding.

4. **Motivate.** Encourage the trainee to perform the job successfully on his or her own. Allow him or her to improve the process or contribute ideas.

5. **Multiply.** Once the trainee is competent and successful, ask him or her to teach others.[45]

It may be desirable or necessary to enlist someone who speaks the employee's native language for the first three steps of this training model, but as we stated earlier, people generally learn more from doing than hearing.

Supervising and Evaluating

❝ People cannot be managed. Inventories can be managed, but people must be led. ❞
—H. Ross Perot

One of the most challenging issues in the workplace is supervising and evaluating job performance of employees. When the employees come from another culture, different viewpoints and expectations about productivity, authority and measures of success can make interacting difficult. The effective manager is sensitive to his or her employees' attitudes and directs them in their work accordingly.

Generally speaking, native-born Americans are taught to be

Latin American and Asian cultures place more emphasis on authority—subordinates wait for instructions and seek approval from their supervisors.

independent and encouraged to make decisions on their own. In the workplace they are often expected to solve problems and complete tasks without much supervision. Managers expect that they can delegate to subordinates and that the job will get done without having to continually check and double-check, and employees seek as much responsibility as possible. Other cultures, particularly Latin American and Asian, place more emphasis on authority—subordinates wait for instructions and seek approval from their supervisors. They may indicate that they understand or agree with a decision even if they don't because they don't want to lose face and because it is disrespectful to challenge a "superior."[46]

When performance is an issue, it is particularly important that managers advise the employee in question about the problem privately. Openly criticizing or patronizing an employee (in any culture) causes embarrassment and considerable loss of face and will generally destroy any chance of mutual respect. It will also result in employees unwilling to risk making mistakes; without risk-taking, there can be no professional growth or skill development.

While it is important that some cultural differences which may pose a problem on the job be addressed (e.g., attitudes about time or a perceived unwillingness to take initiative), managers should remember to separate the behavior from the person. It is common in the United States for an employee to be given a "talking to" by the boss one minute and then go out for a beer together the next. There is a clear separation between the personal and the professional. However, in many cultures, employees identify themselves closely with their job and any criticism of their work is taken both personally and emotionally.

Rather than attack the person, it is important for managers to address the action (or lack of action) and how it affects the running of the business. Focus on the positive by explaining what should be done rather than what shouldn't. For example, Rosa may be late in the mornings because she lives across town and has to get her children to school before leaving for work, but she is nervous about approaching her employer to explain the situation. She is not late because she does not value punctuality, but a lack of clear communication gives her employer that impression. The effective manager would approach Rosa privately and ask her about the situation and be prepared to offer possible ways to solve the problem that are agreeable for both parties (e.g., schedule her for a later shift; exchange break times with later arrival; discover if there is someone with whom she could carpool to work rather than having to take the bus). Do not say, "You're late everyday." Instead try, "Rosa, I've noticed you've been late three mornings this week. I would like to talk about it and come up with ways to help you arrive on time. The doors open at 9:00 and it is important that employees are here to meet our customers."

When delivering criticism, it is helpful to remember the following points:

- Be sincere in wanting to help the employee succeed in his or her job, rather than focusing solely on rules and policies. Show how the employee will benefit from changes as well as how the company will benefit.

- Be specific in describing what needs to be corrected and offer concrete suggestions for improvement. Instead of saying, "I'd like you to work faster." try "I've noticed that you spend about five minutes serving each customer. In order to keep productivity high, we need to serve a customer a minute. Instead of waiting for the order to be ready before taking payment, handle the cash first and get the rest of the order ready while you wait for whatever is being prepared."

- Suggest rather than dictate. Instead of saying "You should…" or "You must…" try "You might want to think about…" or "Let's try to…" (Obvious exceptions to this might include safety regulations: "You must wear a hard hat on site.")

- Invite employees to self-evaluate. Ask them how they feel about certain aspects of their job and how they think they are performing. Also ask them for their input on how to make changes.

- Set goals for improvement and achievable measurements of success.

- Build trust by admitting your own mistakes. "When I started this company, I couldn't work the phone properly and hung up on all of my customers, so I understand your difficulty with the new system."

- "Walk the talk." To maintain credibility, effective managers and employers practice what they preach to employees. If punctuality is a problem for an employee, the boss had better not be late. If employees are expected to be upbeat and friendly, demonstrate enthusiasm and lead by example.

It is also important to counter any negative feelings, wounded pride, etc., by reassuring and praising employees for the good work they are doing separate from the problem area. A genuine and specific comment such as "I really appreciate your friendly manner with our guests; it really makes our customer service stand out above the competition." is much more valued than "Good job."

Rewarding Success

Success usually comes to those who are too busy to be looking for it.
—Henry David Thoreau

Employee incentives can often go a long way in motivating people to do their best. Some people are intrinsically motivated to do a great job, but most people (in all cultures) require some kind of recognition or reward for positive contributions to their company.

Employee-of-the-Month programs, Achievement Certificates and other short-term incentives for personal contributions or teamwork are appreciated, but rewards that reflect appreciation for the individual's hard work may also be welcomed, such as:

- A framed picture of the employee on the job (with co-workers if employee is conscious about being singled out).

- Pre-paid telephone cards for people to call their relatives in their country of origin.

- A subscription to a daily newspaper from their home country (or from the United States if the person has a specific hobby or interest).

- A personal thank you note in the employee's first language.

- Recognition of a national holiday in the employee's home country (a flag, pin or poster from the consulate or embassy— see Appendix B for Independence Days of various nations).

- Company clothing or promotional items (T-shirts, hats, pens, tote bags, etc.) with employee's name or initial.

In the Chinese culture it is considered bad luck to receive a clock as a gift.

Where gift-giving is concerned, there are cultural considerations to be made so employers should investigate what might be thought of as inappropriate by particular employees. In the Chinese culture, for example, it is considered bad luck to receive a clock as a gift. Also, cut flowers are related to funerals and green hats are ill-advised (a man who "wears a green hat" is being betrayed by his wife). Also, it is not a good idea to wrap a gift in white paper; white is also associated with death and funerals.[47]

Other forms of reward and encouragement include wealth-building programs such as stock options and profit sharing, as well as real opportunities for skill development and career advancement. Non-financial incentives such as being able to work in a dynamic and enjoyable environment also go a long way toward encouraging employees to give their best. Another appreciated gesture is the recognition of achievements or important life events outside of work (e.g., finishing a diploma or degree after months or years of night school, running a marathon, having a baby.) Employers need to think about what it is they want to achieve as a company and how to measure and reward success. What is rewarded and recognized communicates what is valued.[48]

Managing Conflict

> *Discussion is an exchange of knowledge; argument an exchange of ignorance.*
> —Robert Quillen

Just as there are different styles of communication, so are there different ways of handling conflict. Some people get angry or upset and argue; others withdraw into stony silence. Still others consider conflict a healthy aspect of communication that motivates us to act (or not act). Conflict is often a constructive way to challenge established norms and practices and can enable us to be our most creative and innovative.[49] Our culture as well as our personality determines whether or not we think of conflict as a productive process or a threatening event.

Our culture as well as our personality determines whether or not we think of conflict as a productive process or a threatening event.

For conflict to occur, one person's or group's goals must not only be incompatible with those of another, but there must also be a mutual stake and some sort of interaction involved. If my goal is to sell top-quality discount shoes and the neighboring business's interest is surfboards, there is no conflict. If, however, the manager of the neighboring business takes my parking spot every morning, then there is conflict. We both want the same thing (a parking spot) and there are consequences for each of us if the other "wins" the dispute (one of us will have to walk farther or possibly pay more for another spot). If the other manager comes from a different cultural background, the conflict might escalate because her way of looking at the situation is different from mine. Coming from a low-context culture, I would likely wait for an appropriate moment, state directly that she is parking in a reserved place and request that she move her vehicle. If she is from a high-context culture, she may not feel comfortable approaching me (or being approached directly) to discuss it. Perhaps she isn't aware of other parking options or doesn't understand that "Reserved" means that she can't park there.

Note: While violence is not considered an acceptable way of handling conflict, it is nonetheless a last resort (or first option) in many cultures. In terms of interpersonal communication, we will work with the assumption that physical aggression and verbal abuse are not appropriate or productive means of resolving issues or disputes.

Resolving conflict—between management and staff or among

employees themselves—requires significant time and commitment from all of the parties involved. Participants in all sides of the disagreement, especially managers, need to be open to more than one possible solution and prepared to implement one or several in order to resolve the problem. One process of conflict resolution includes the following steps:

1. **Identification.** Each side needs to be able to identify the problem from their own point of view without being blamed, judged or interrupted. Each person's needs, interests and positions should be clarified. When all concerns are aired, disagreeing parties should be asked to paraphrase what they heard to ensure they really understood the other perspective(s). Finally, a "nutshell" definition, in specific and neutral terms, of the underlying issue should be agreed upon by all parties. If the situation is particularly volatile, an outside mediator (preferably who speaks the languages of the parties involved) would be helpful in trying to help opposing sides find a common ground.

2. **Suggestions.** At this stage, any and all possible ways to resolve the issue should be generated by the parties involved, without evaluating them. This can be done in a group "brainstorm" with random ideas written onto a white board. Or, if there are two opposing "camps," each side may be asked to make a list of what the other side should do and then exchange lists. Keep in mind that there are different cultural approaches to solving a problem that may not show an obvious cause-and-effect pattern. For example, someone might illustrate a solution by describing a seemingly unrelated story or giving a metaphor with a "hidden" meaning. Keep an open mind.

3. **Assessment.** Each proposed alternative should be discussed and weighed according to how successful it might be in resolving the issue for all parties and still meet company goals.

Possible outcomes may, and likely will, require compromise from all sides. Allow people to save face by emphasizing that being able to change your position shows strength and professionalism.

4. **Decision.** The solution agreed upon by all parties should be specifically stated and a plan made to put it into practice—the details of who will do what, when and how should be clearly defined. All parties agree to participate in the solution and someone is designated to ensure the plan is put into action and monitor progress.

5. **Implementation.** The plan is carried out by all parties. If progress is not being made in a reasonable interval of time (decided by the participants in the decision-making stage), then the process should be repeated, applying another suggested solution to the problem.

Saying No

" *Yes and no are the oldest and simplest words, but they require the most thought.*
—*Pythagorus*

It is unrealistic to expect that all communication will always be positive. Even the best managers (and employees) encounter situations where they will have to deal with refusal (either giving or receiving). However, managers and employers should be sensitive to the fact that saying no in some cultures is difficult or just not done at all. For example, in China it is considered unacceptably rude to flatly refuse a request made by a guest or a superior. Being polite and maintaining harmony always supercede the desire to say no, complain or disagree. Rather than say an outright no to an impossible request, it is more acceptable to say that something is "inconvenient" or "under consideration," or simply say nothing at all.[50]

To apply an example of this cultural difference to a small business setting in the United States, a manager may assign a particular project or task to an employee of, for example, Chinese descent. He or she may accept the task even if it is beyond his or her power to complete due to training, time constraints or unclear expectations in order to save face and not appear to be unmotivated or shirking responsibilities. However, a careful interpretation of his or her reaction (e.g., hesitation or silence or other subtle signals) when given the job would have shown a deep reluctance to take it on. A sensitive manager would take the correct cue and probe for more information or offer to find ways to help complete the task.

Similarly, if that same employee makes a request of management that is difficult or impossible to grant, it may be considered unduly harsh or critical to dismiss it out of hand. While "delay tactics" such as "I'll think about that and get back to you." may seem dishonest or inconvenient to a native-born American, to others it may be construed as a polite refusal that allows all parties to save face.

It is important to find out how disagreement is handled in other cultures and equally important to double-check "agreements" to ensure that both parties are on the same wavelength.

Managing Attitudes and Behavior

" *Maybe the truest thing to be said about racism is that it represents a profound failure of the imagination.* "
—Henry Louis Gates, Jr.

In order for a diverse workplace to function well, all employees must feel safe, valued and respected. Managers and employers have an obligation—legally and morally—to ensure that no one is subjected to insulting or threatening language, labels or behavior in the workplace. Inappropriate behavior is often ignored because it is easier to "let it go" than confront the offender. People are afraid of being seen as paranoid or "poor sports" if they take offence. However, an employer that tolerates or condones harassment (in any form) runs the risk of liability because ultimately he or she controls the work environment and is responsible for it. It is critical that both managers and employees address offensive comments and make it clear that they are unacceptable. One effective way to do this is a four-step process, suggested by Lenora Billings-Harris in her book *The Diversity Advantage*, called S.T.O.P.

S = State the behavior objectively.

T = Tell the offender how you feel when he or she acts or speaks that way.

O = Options: offer alternative behaviors that are acceptable.

P = Positive results: give a reason for changing the behavior.

For example, several co-workers are gathered around the coffee machine discussing current events in the Middle East. One person refers to an Arab co-worker as "Osama bin Laden." Although the co-worker did not hear the slur, you rightly feel obligated to address the comment. Wait until that person is alone and ask to speak to them for a moment. Your comments might go something like this: "John, earlier at the coffee machine you referred to (Name) as Osama bin Laden. (S) It makes me very uncomfortable that you would use that name for a co-worker based on his ethnic origin. (T) I would prefer if you would address colleagues by their actual names and avoid references that are likely to insult them. (O) The awkwardness and tension that is created by labeling people will disappear in the office and your insights on current events will be welcomed. (P) I appreciate your efforts in making this a comfortable place to work for everyone in the company."

Putting this method into action takes some practice and it may not have an immediate or obvious effect other than to shock the other person into silence. The purpose is to get your point across quickly and non-judgmentally. It may be helpful if you plan what you want to say ahead of time and practice the method until you become comfortable with it.[51]

Obviously, one of the best ways for managers to ensure that the workplace is free from offensive language and behavior is to model appropriate attitudes and actions themselves. Earlier, the importance of language and its effect on others was discussed. It is easy to assume that the words we choose are the correct ones because we don't mean to offend, but others may be offended nonetheless.

Several writers about diversity suggest that managers address this problem by asking employees directly what is and is not acceptable to them. (For example, some Americans with Latino heritage object to the word Hispanic and others do not.) Ask employees to develop a list of preferred terms and usage, then post the list as well as circulate it to the staff individually. Periodically revisit the list because what is "appropriate" changes regularly. Additional points to remember:

- Do not use slang terms or derogatory expressions when referring to others.

- Do not allow employees to circulate racist or offensive material via e-mail.

- Respect personal names. Find out the polite way to address a person (e.g., by family name, by first name, or by last name first) as well as proper pronunciation and spelling.

- Be willing to apologize if you have given offense.

- It is not acceptable to make jokes or derogatory comments about others from a different cultural or ethnic group or about people with differences (e.g., physical challenges) even if they do about themselves.

- Do not assume that people want to be identified as belonging to a certain cultural group or ethnicity. Deal with people as individuals rather than as representatives of a particular group unless requested to do so.

- When in doubt, ask.

Team-Building

" *By working together, pooling our resources and building on our strengths, we can accomplish great things.* "
—*Ronald Reagan*

A large part of successfully communicating with a diverse group of employees involves team-building. A "group" is just several people in the same place; a "team" is several people with the same goal. People simply working together under the same roof or for the same company do not necessarily share the same goals, especially when they have diverse needs, expectations and abilities. A team has a common purpose and the combined efforts of all of the participants working together lead to success for individuals and the company as a whole.

Strong teams are comprised of several elements. Every member understands what is important to the team and how they contribute to the common goal. Every member understands that his or her contribution is valuable and necessary for the effective functioning of the team. Every member trusts that everyone else is doing their best. Every member respects and cooperates with the rest of the team. Every member is committed to the team and is prepared to make personal sacrifices to reach the goal. Every member is prepared to assume different roles when necessary to achieve success.

The key to all of these elements is communication. Team members must be free and safe to openly communicate with each other as well as with management to build trust, to learn and to progress. It doesn't happen automatically—managers and employers have to lead the way.

Managers can facilitate team-building and the development of trust in many ways.

- Organize regular opportunities for people to learn something new together. Sponsor workshops or training sessions; change the group members so that different people get to relate with each other. Ask one member of the group to teach to the rest; rotate teachers so everyone learns from everyone else.

- Organize social and sporting events both at and after work. Invite the team for a monthly breakfast or barbecue. Have a weekly lunchtime volleyball game. Allow opportunities for shared "fun."

- Adopt a charity and encourage employees to participate in community service. Enter the team in a fundraising sporting event; sponsor a family as a group for the holidays.

- Organize annual events that involve family members. Rent a skating rink for an afternoon or spend a day at a theme park.

- Provide employees with company clothing and paraphernalia. Wearing the company logo instills pride and a sense of belonging.

- Institute a suggestion box and make a regular and committed effort to recognize and discuss suggestions. Reward people for their good ideas.

- Encourage employees to recognize their co-workers. It is very rewarding to be noticed by peers as well as by superiors, contributing to a greater sense of commitment to the team.

- Show an interest in employees' family members and make them feel welcome in the workplace. Encourage staff to display family photos. In a family-friendly company, the company becomes an extension of the family itself.

- Design a company Web site (or add a link to your existing site) and post employee news—personal milestones or events, team-building activities, corporate information, etc.—in the language(s) of your employees.

- Make the staffroom or lunch corner a comfortable, welcoming place for all employees. It goes without saying that pin-up calendars are not appropriate wall art, but a decent coat of paint, some plants and a tidy atmosphere in which to enjoy

breaks and meals will make employees feel appreciated.
Institute a rotating schedule of clean-up duty so employees take
ownership of their surroundings.

- Practice "management by walking around." Spend part of
each day circulating among staff, following up on questions
or concerns, giving encouragement. Not only will you stay
up to date on what is happening with your employees both
professionally and personally, you will also demonstrate an
open line of communication.

Communication and Collaboration

"Alone we can do so little, together we can do so much."
—Helen Keller

As this book has attempted to discuss, communication is the driving
force behind successfully managing employees of diverse cultural and
linguistic backgrounds. Communication is inextricably tied to culture:
our culture informs how we think and interact with others. True
and positive communication can only occur when people of different
cultures stretch their awareness of the other's attitudes and behavior.
Understanding generates respect and a willingness to collaborate to
achieve a common purpose: success.

Spanish-speaking and Asian employees, as groups and as individuals
within those groups, have unique perspectives to bring to the
American workplace. It is the responsibility of the employer to
discover what those perspectives are and how to apply them to their
own business to maximize the benefits to the company and the

employee. Managing a diverse workforce is a long-term process for developing an environment that works for all employees and allows the people being managed to reach their full potential.[52] It requires enabling employees to do their jobs using their full range of skills and talents. It requires recognizing individual strengths and weaknesses and helping employees improve both. It requires acknowledging and accommodating cultural differences and valuing those differences as avenues for growth and success for the company.

Most of all, managing a diverse workforce requires adaptability. Managers and employers of foreign-born workers need to be aware of and use different approaches to communicate effectively. They need to be sensitive to differences between cultures as well as to their own biases. They need to be able to step into another person's cultural shoes and adjust their thinking in order to build trust, earn respect and secure loyalty. The only way to do this is through a continuous, open, two-way dialogue utilizing conscious and varied methods of verbal and non-verbal communication. Positive and healthy interaction demonstrates a respect for the individual and appreciation of his or her contribution to the company. The investment of time and effort in meeting these challenges will pay huge dividends in increased productivity, creative problem-solving and effective teamwork. The end result is a strong and vibrant company.

APPENDIX A

Job Interviews and Employment Applications

" Judge of a man by his questions rather than by his answers."
—*Voltaire*

Unacceptable Questions

(Source: Adapted from material in Gómez-Mejía et al. *Managing Human Resources*, 3rd ed. Upper Saddle River, NJ: Prentice Hall, 2001, pp. 114-115)

- ***What is your maiden name?***
  (You may not ask questions relating to marital status or national origin.)

- ***How old are you? What is your date of birth?***
  (You may ask if the person is at least 18 and ask if they are willing to show legal proof of age if hired.)

- *What is your race? Where do you come from?*
  (You may not ask questions relating to race or ethnicity.)

- *Are you an American citizen?*
  (You may ask if a person is legally allowed to work in the United States; e.g., have a work visa.)

- *What is your sex? Are you married?*
  (You may not ask questions relating to gender or marital status.)

- *Do you have children? Do you have reliable child care? Are you planning to get pregnant?*
  (You may not ask direct or indirect questions related to family as they may be considered discriminatory against women.)

- *What is your height/weight?*
  (You may not ask questions relating to physical characteristics.)

- *Please submit a photograph with your application.*
  (You may require a photo for ID purposes when hired, but cannot ask for one beforehand.)

- *What language do you speak at home?*
  (You may ask if they speak, read or write a foreign language.)

- *Do you have any mental or physical disabilities, or illnesses (including AIDS or HIV)?*
  (You may not ask questions regarding physical ability, but you may ask if the person is willing to take a physical exam if it can be proven that the job requires one.)

- *What is your religion?*
  (You may not ask about religious affiliation, but you may ask if a person is available to work certain times and days of the week.)

- **Please list any/all hobbies you have or organizations to which you belong.**
  (You may ask if the person has interests or memberships in organizations that would relate to the job, but you should inform the person they do not have to include those that are associated with age, race, sex or religion.)

- **Do you own your home or rent? Do you own your own car?**
  (You may not ask questions related to a person's credit rating, but you may ask if a person has access to a vehicle if the job requires it.)

- **Have you ever been arrested for a crime?**
  (You may ask if a person has ever been convicted of a crime.)

As of September 30, 2002, the permanent federal workforce included 113,418 Hispanics (6.9 percent), as compared to 107,267 Hispanics (6.6 percent) a year earlier, representing an increase of 6,151 (5.7 percent).

—*Source: Statistical Information on Hispanic Employment in Federal Agencies,*

Report To The President, June 2003

" Everything that is really great and inspiring is created by the individual who can labor in freedom."

—*Albert Einstein*

The following charts contain the Independence Days for Latin, America, South America and Asia. Be aware that these days can hold very special meaning for your employees.

Latin America/South America

(Source: *Thomas, Jennifer, Spanish for Hospitality and Foodservice,* p. 270. Upper Saddle River, NJ: Pearson-Prentice Hall, 2004.)

Country	Independence Day
Argentina	July 9
Bolivia	August 6
Chile	September 18
Colombia	July 20
Costa Rica	September 15
Cuba	May 20
Dominican Republic	February 22
Ecuador	October 3
El Salvador	September 15
Guatemala	September 15
Honduras	September 15
Mexico	September 16
Nicaragua	September 15
Panama	November 28 (from Spain)
	November 3 (from Colombia)
Paraguay	May 14
Peru	July 28
Uruguay	August 25
Venezuela	July 5

Asia

(Source: CIA—The World Factbook on the Internet: www.cia.gov/cia /publications/factbook/geos/kn.html.)

Country	Independence Day
Afghanistan	August 19
Cambodia	November 9
China	October 1
(National Day: founding of People's Republic of China)	
India	August 15
Indonesia	August 17
Japan	February 11 (National Foundation Day)
Laos	July 19 (from France)
	December 2 (Republic Day)
Malaysia	April 30
Myanmar (Burma)	January 4
North Korea	August 15 (from Japan)
	September 9
(founding of Democratic People's Republic of Korea)	
Pakistan	August 14
Philippines	June 12
South Korea	August 15
Taiwan	October 10 (Republic Day)
Thailand	December 5 (King's birthday)
Vietnam	September 2

Central Asia

East Asia

Latin & South America

GLOSSARY

Common Workplace Terminology

"The words that enlighten the soul are more precious than jewels."
—Hazrat Inayat Khan

PRONOUNS	PRONOMBRES	代名词
I, me	Yo, yo	我，我
we	Nosotros	我们
he	él	你们
she	ella	他
it	ello	它
they, them	ellos	他们，他们
this	este	这
that	aquel	那
one	uno, un	一

POSSESSIVES	PRONOMBRES POSESIVOS	所有格
mine	mío	我的

our, ours	nuestro, nuestra	我们的, 我们的
your, yours	tuyo, vuestro	你们的, 你们的
his	suyo	他的
hers	suya	她的
its	suyo, suya	它的
their	sus	他们的
theirs	suyos, suyas	他们的

GETTING ACQUAINTED   SIENDO PRESENTADO

Hi!	Hola!	嗨!
How are you?	¿Cómo estás?	你好
I'm fine, thanks.	Bien, gracias.	我很好，谢谢.
Good morning.	Buen día.	早上好
Good afternoon.	Buenas tardes.	下午好
Good evening.	Buenas noches.	晚上好
Goodnight.	Buenas noches.	晚安
Hello, I am _____.	Hola, yo soy _____.	喂, 我是 _____.
My name is _____.	Mi nombre es_____.	我的名字叫 ____.
This is ___.	Esto es _____.	这是 ____.
What's your name?	¿Cuál es tu nombre?	你叫什么名字?
Welcome.	Bienvenido.	欢迎.
It's nice to meet you.	Es un gusto conocerte.	很高兴见到你.
I am pleased to meet you.	Estoy encantado de conocerte.	我很高兴见到你
It was nice meeting you.	Fue lindo conocerte.	见到你很高兴.
Where are you from?	¿De dónde eres?	你从那里来?
I come from ___.	Yo vengo de_____.	我来自 ____.
What do you do?	¿Qué haces?	你作什么的?

I am a _____., I work as a _____.
 Yo soy _____, trabajo como _____.   我是一个 ___., 我是一位 ____.

How do you like ____?   ¿ Cómo te gustan_____?   你觉得怎么样__?

When did you come to _____?
 ¿ Cuándo fuiste a _____?   你会什么时候做 _____?

It's a nice/warm/cold day.
 Es un día agradable/cálido/frío.   这是舒适/暖和/寒冷的一天.

Make yourself comfortable.	Ponte cómodo.	不要拘束.
May I take your coat?	¿Puedo tomar su saco?	我可以拿你的外套吗?
Please sit down.	Por favor siéntese.	请坐下.
Do you speak English?	¿Hablas inglés?	你说英语吗?
Yes, I do.	Si.	是的, 我说.
Can you read English?	¿Puedes leer en inglés?	你能读英语吗?
No, I can't.	No, no puedo.	不, 我不能.
Do you understand?	¿Entiendes?	你明白吗?
A little.	Un poquito.	一点点.
I don't understand.	No entiendo.	我不明白.

Please speak more slowly.
 Por favor, hábleme mas lento.   请慢一点说.

Can you repeat that?	¿Puede repetir eso?	你能重复吗?
How do you say _____?	¿Cómo dices_____?	你说的怎样?
Good-bye.	Adiós.	再见.
See you later.	Nos vemos luego.	待会见.
See you tomorrow.	Nos vemos mañana.	明天见.
Have a good night.	Que tengas una buena noche.	晚上愉快.
Congratulations.	Felicitaciones.	祝贺.
Happy birthday.	Feliz Cumpleaños.	生日快乐.
Happy anniversary.	Feliz Aniversario.	周年快乐.
Are you ready to go?	¿Estás listo para irte?	你准备好了吗?
Let's go.	Vamos.	走吧.

POLITE WORDS   PALABRAS DE CORTESÍA.

Please	Por favor.	请

Thank you. Thanks.	Gracias a usted, Gracias.	谢谢你, 谢谢.
Thank you very much.	Muchas gracias.	非常感谢你.
Excuse me.	Discúlpeme.	对不起.
You're welcome.	De nada.	欢迎你.
It's no trouble.	No es problema.	没有问题
May I help you?	¿Puedo ayudarlo?	我能帮助你吗?
I'm sorry.	Discúlpeme.	我抱歉.
Pardon me.	Perdóneme.	原谅我.
I beg your pardon?	¿Cómo dice?	我请你原谅?
That's okay.	Esta bien.	好的
No problem.	No hay problema.	没有问题
Of course.	Por supuesto.	当然.
Don't worry about it.	No se preocupe por eso.	不必担心.
Bless you!	¡salud!	祝福你!
Have a nice day!	¡Que tengas un buen día !	过快乐的一天!
Sure.	Seguro.	当然.
Go ahead.	Adelante.	前进.
It's my pleasure.	Es un placer.	我高兴.

QUESTIONS   PREGUNTAS

Who?	¿Quién?	谁?
Whose?	¿De quién?	谁的
What?	¿Qué?	什么?
What kind?	¿De que clase?	什么类型的?
When?	¿Cuándo?	什么时候?
Where?	¿Dónde?	什么地方?
Which?	¿Cuál?	那一个?
Why?	¿Por qué?	为什么
How?	¿Cómo?	怎么?
How much?	¿Cuánto?	多少?
How many?	¿Cuántos?	多少?
How do you say ___?	¿Cómo dices ____?	你怎样说 ____?
What does this mean?	¿Qué significa esto?	这意味着什么?
Are you okay?	¿Estás bien?	你好了吗?

Are you sick?	¿Estás enfermo?	你病了吗?
What's the matter?	¿Qué pasa?	什么问题?
Can you tell me?	¿Puedes decirme?	你能告诉我吗?
What do you want to know?	¿Qué quieres saber?	你想知道什么?
What happened?	¿Qué pasó?	发生什么了?
Where did it happen?	¿Dónde pasó?	什么地方发生的?
When did it happen?	¿Cuándo pasó?	什么时候发生的?
How can I help you?	¿Cómo puedo ayudarte?	我怎样帮助你?
Do you need help?	¿Necesita ayuda?	你需要帮助吗?

DAYS OF THE WEEK	**DÍAS DE LA SEMANA**	星期
Monday	Lunes	星期一
Tuesday	Martcs	星期二
Wednesday	Miércoles	星期三
Thursday	Jueves	星期四
Friday	Viernes	星期五
Saturday	Sábado	星期六
Sunday	Domingo	星期天

MONTHS OF THE YEAR	**MESES DEL AÑO**	月份
January	Enero	一月
February	Febrero	二月
March	Marzo	三月
April	Abril	四月
May	Mayo	五月
June	Junio	六月
July	Julio	七月
August	Agosto	八月
September	Septiembre	九月
October	Octubre	十月
November	Noviembre	十一月
December	Diciembre	十二月

SEASONS	ESTACIONES	季节
spring	primavera	春天
summer	verano	夏天
fall, autumn	otoño	秋天
winter	invierno	冬天

WEATHER/TEMPERATURE	TIEMPO/TEMPERATURA	天气/温度
bright	brillante	晴
cloudy	nublado	多云
cold	frío	冷
cool	fresco	凉爽
dark	oscuro	
drizzle	llovizna	小雨
earthquake	terremoto	地震
flood, flooding	inundación, inundado	洪水
fog, foggy	niebla, nebuloso	雾
freezing	con temperaturas bajo cero	冰冻
frost, frosty	helado	霜冻
hot	calor	热
humid, humidity	humedad, húmedo	潮湿
light	luz	阳光
lightning	luminoso	阳光
rainy, raining	lluvioso, lloviendo	多雨
snowing	nevando	雪
storm, stormy	tormenta, tormentoso	暴风雨
sunny	soleado	晴
thunder	trueno	打雷
tornado	tornado	龙卷风
warm	cálido	温暖的

PREPOSITIONS	PREPOSICIONES	前置词
above	encima de	在...上面

beneath	bajo	在 ...下面
beside	al lado de	在旁边
between	entre	在中间
by	junto a	经，由
during	durante	在...期间
for	por, para	为了,因为,至于,对于,适合于
from	desde	从,今后,来自,由于
in	en	.在...之内
near	cerca	.在...近旁,近
of	de	...的,由...制成的,离,关于,对于
on	sobre	在..之上
over	encima de	结束
through	a través	通过
under	bajo	在...之下
until	hasta	到...为止
with	con	用，由于
without	sin	没有

CONJUNCTIONS / CONJUNCIONES / 关联词

although	Aunque	尽管
and	y	和，与
because	porque	因为
but	pero	但是
if	si	如果
that	aquel	在
therefore	entonces	因此，所以
when	cuando	当，在...时候
where	donde	在那里，什么地方
yet	aún	仍然

LOCATION WORDS / PALABRAS DE UBICACIÓN / 位置词汇

anywhere	cualquier sitio	无论何处
away from	lejos de	远离
close to	cerca de	接近于,在附近

everywhere	por todos lados	各处, 到处
far	lejos	久远的
here	aquí	在这里
in	en	在...之内
inside	dentro	里面
near	cerca	在...旁边, 近
next to	próximo a	几乎
out	fuera	外边的
outside	exterior	外边, 外表
somewhere	algún lugar	某处
there	ahí	在那里

DIRECTIONS   DIRECCIONES   方向

east	este	东方, 东
west	oeste	西方, 西
north	norte	北方, 北
south	sur	南方, 南
northeast	noreste	东北
northwest	noroeste	西北
southeast	sudeste	东南
southwest	sudoeste	西南
Go straight.	Siga derecho.	笔直走

Turn left at the lights.
    Doble a la izquierda en el semáforo.   在那些灯旁向左拐.

Turn right at the corner.
    Doble a la derecha en la esquina.   在角落向右拐.

Walk for _ blocks.
    Camine _ cuadras.   走 _ 块.

It is across the street from__.
    Está cruzando la calle desde__.   通过另一边街道过来__.

Take the next street.

Tome la próxima calle.   到下一街道.

NUMBERS	NÚMEROS	数字
one (1)	uno (1)	一 (1)
two (2)	dos (2)	二 (2)
three (3)	tres (3)	三 (3)
four (4)	cuatro (4)	四 (4)
five (5)	cinco (5)	五 (5)
six (6)	seis (6)	六 (6)
seven (7)	siete (7)	七 (7)
eight (8)	ocho (8)	八 (8)
nine (9)	nueve (9)	九 (9)
ten (10)	diez (10)	十 (10)
eleven (11)	once (11)	十一 (11)
twelve (12)	doce (12)	十二 (12)
thirteen (13)	trece (13)	十三 (13)
fourteen (14)	catorce (14)	十四 (14)
fifteen (15)	quince (15)	十五 (15)
sixteen (16)	dieciséis (16)	十六 (16)
seventeen (17)	diecisietc (17)	十七 (17)
eighteen (18)	dieciocho (18)	十八 (18)
nineteen (19)	diecinucve (19)	十九 (19)
twenty (20)	veinte (20)	二十 (20)
twenty-one (21)	veintiuno (21)	二十一 (21)
twenty-two (22)	veintidós (22)	二十二 (22)
twenty-three (23)	veintitrés (23)	二十三 (23)
twenty-four (24)	veinticuatro (24)	二十四 (24)
twenty-five (25)	veinticinco (25)	二十五 (25)
twenty-six (26)	veintiséis (26)	二十六 (26)
twenty-seven (27)	veintisiete (27)	二十七 (27)
twenty-eight (28)	veintiocho (28)	二十八 (28)
twenty-nine (29)	veintinueve (29)	二十九 (29)
thirty (30)	treinta (30)	三十 (30)

thirty-one (31)	treinta y uno (31)	三十一 (31)
thirty-two (32)	treinta y dos (32)	三十二 (32)
thirty-three (33)	treinta y tres (33)	三十三 (33)
thirty-four (34)	treinta y cuatro (34)	三十四 (34)
thirty-five (35)	treinta y cinco (35)	三十五 (35)
thirty-six (36)	treinta y seis (36)	三十六 (36)
thirty-seven (37)	treinta y siete (37)	三十七 (37)
thirty-eight (38)	treinta y ocho (38)	三十八 (38)
thirty-nine (39)	treinta y nueve (39)	三十九 (39)
forty (40)	cuarenta (40)	四十 (40)
forty-one (41)	cuarenta y uno (41)	四十一 (41)
forty-two (42)	cuarenta y dos (42)	四十二 (42)
forty-three (43)	cuarenta y tres (43)	四十三 (43)
forty-four (44)	cuarenta y cuatro (44)	四十四 (44)
forty-five (45)	cuarenta y cinco (45)	四十五 (45)
forty-six (46)	cuarenta y seis (46)	四十六 (46)
forty-seven (47)	cuarenta y siete (47)	四十七 (47)
forty-eight (48)	cuarenta y ocho (48)	四十八 (48)
forty-nine (49)	cuarenta y nueve (49)	四十九 (49)
fifty (50)	cincuenta (50)	五十 (50)
fifty-one (51)	cincuenta y uno (51)	五十一 (51)
fifty-two (52)	cincuenta y dos (52)	五十二 (52)
fifty-three (53)	cincuenta y tres (53)	五十三 (53)
fifty-four (54)	cincuenta y cuatro (54)	五十四 (54)
fifty-five (55)	cincuenta y cinco (55)	五十五 (55)
fifty-six (56)	cincuenta y seis (56)	五十六 (56)
fifty-seven (57)	cincuenta y siete (57)	五十七 (57)
fifty-eight (58)	cincuenta y ocho (58)	五十八 (58)
fifty-nine (59)	cincuenta y nueve (59)	五十九 (59)
sixty (60)	sesenta (60)	六十 (60)
sixty-one (61)	sesenta y uno (61)	六十一 (61)
sixty-two (62)	sesenta y dos (62)	六十二 (62)
sixty-three (63)	sesenta y tres (63)	六十三 (63)
sixty-four (64)	sesenta y cuatro (64)	六十四 (64)
sixty-five (65)	sesenta y cinco (65)	六十五 (65)
sixty-six (66)	sesenta y seis (66)	六十六 (66)

sixty-seven (67)	sesenta y siete (67)	六十七 (67)
sixty-eight (68)	sesenta y ocho (68)	六十八 (68)
sixty-nine (69)	sesenta y nueve (69)	六十九 (69)
seventy (70)	setenta (70)	七十 (70)
seventy-one (71)	setenta y uno (71)	七十一 (71)
seventy-two (72)	setenta y dos (72)	七十二 (72)
seventy-three (73)	setenta y tres (73)	七十三 (73)
seventy-four (74)	setenta y cuatro (74)	七十四 (74)
seventy-five (75)	setenta y cinco (75)	七十五 (75)
seventy-six (76)	setenta y seis (76)	七十六 (76)
seventy-seven (77)	setenta y siete (77)	七十七 (77)
seventy-eight (78)	setenta y ocho (78)	七十八 (78)
seventy-nine (79)	setenta y nueve (79)	七十九 (79)
eighty (80)	ochenta (80)	八十 (80)
eighty-one (81)	ochenta y uno (81)	八十一 (81)
eighty-two (82)	ochenta y dos (82)	八十二 (82)
eighty-three (83)	ochenta y tres (83)	八十三 (83)
eighty-four (84)	ochenta y cuatro (84)	八十四 (84)
eighty-five (85)	ochenta y cinco (85)	八十五 (85)
eighty-six (86)	ochenta y seis (86)	八十六 (86)
eighty-seven (87)	ochenta y siete (87)	八十七 (87)
eighty-eight (88)	ochenta y ocho (88)	八十八 (88)
eighty-nine (89)	ochenta y nueve (89)	八十九 (89)
einety (90)	noventa (90)	九十 (90)
ninety-one (91)	noventa y uno (91)	九十一 (91)
ninety-two (92)	noventa y dos (92)	九十二 (92)
ninety-three (93)	noventa y tres (93)	九十三 (93)
ninety-four (94)	noventa y cuatro (94)	九十四 (94)
ninety-five (95)	noventa y cinco (95)	九十五 (95)
ninety-six (96)	noventa y seis (96)	九十六 (96)
ninety-seven (97)	noventa y siete (97)	九十七 (97)
ninety-eight (98)	noventa y ocho (98)	九十八 (98)
ninety-nine (99)	noventa y nueve (99)	九十九 (99)
one hundred (100)	cien (100)	一百 (100)
two hundred (200)	doscientos (200)	两百 (200)
three hundred (300)	trescientos (300)	三百 (300)

four hundred (400)	cuatrocientos (400)	三百(400)
five hundred (500)	quinientos (500)	三百 (500)
six hundred (600)	seiscientos (600)	三百 (600)
seven hundred (700)	setecientos (700)	三百 (700)
eight hundred (800)	ochocientos (800)	三百 (800)
nine hundred (900)	novecientos (900)	三百 (900)
one thousand (1,000)	mil (1,000)	三百 (1,000)
ten thousand (10,000)	diez mil (10,000)	三百(10,000)

one hundred thousand (100,000)
    cien mil (100,000)   十万 (100,000)

one million (1,000, 000)
    un millón (1,000,000)   一百万 (1,000,000)

one billion (1,000,000,000)
    un billón (1,000,000,000)   十亿(1,000,000,000)

one trillion (1,000,000,000,000)
    un trillón (1,000,000,000,000)   一万亿 (1,000,000,000,000)

one-sixteenth (1/16)	un décimo sexto (1/16)	十六分之一 (1/16)
one-eighth (1/8)	un octavo (1/8)	八分之一 (1/8)
one-quarter (1/4)	un cuarto (1/4)	四分之一(1/4)
one-half (1/2)	una mitad (1/2)	二分之一 (1/2)
one-third (1/3)	un tercio (1/3)	三分之一 (1/3)
three-quarters (3/4)	tres cuartos (3/4)	四分之三 (3/4)
first	primero	第一
second	segundo	第二
third	tercero	第三
fourth	cuarto	第四
fifth	quinto	第五
sixth	sexto	第六
seventh	séptimo	第七
eighth	octavo	第八
ninth	noveno	第九

tenth	décimo	第十
eleventh	décimoprimero	第十一
twelfth	décimosegundo	第十二
thirteenth	décimotercero	第十三
fourteenth	décimocuarto	第十四
fifteenth	décimoquinto	第十五
sixteenth	décimosexto	第十六
seventeenth	décimoséptimo	第十七
eighteenth	décimo octavo	第十八
nineteenth	décimo noveno	第十九
twentieth	vigésimo	第二十

TIME WORDS PALABRAS DEL TIEMPO 时间词汇

one o'clock (1:00)	una en punto (1:00)	一点钟 (1:00)
two o'clock (2:00)	dos en punto (2:00)	二点钟 (2:00)
three o'clock (3:00)	tres en punto (3:00)	三点钟 (3:00)
four o'clock (4:00)	cuatro en punto (4:00)	四点钟 (4:00)
five o'clock (5:00)	cinco en punto (5:00)	五点钟 (5:00)
six o'clock (6:00)	seis en punto (6:00)	六点钟 (6:00)
seven o'clock (7:00)	siete en punto (7:00)	七点钟 (7:00)
eight o'clock (8:00)	ocho en punto (8:00)	八点钟 (8:00)
nine o'clock (9:00)	nueve en punto (9:00)	九钟 (9:00)
ten o'clock (10:00)	diez en punto (10:00)	十点钟 (10:00)
eleven o'clock (11:00)	once en punto (11:00)	十一点钟 (11:00)
twelve o'clock (12:00)	doce en punto (12:00)	十二点钟 (12:00)

a quarter past, a quarter after (--:15)
y cuarto pasadas, un cuarto después (--:15) 过十五分钟 (--:15)

a quarter of, a quarter to (--:45)
un cuarto para las (--:45) 四十五分钟 (--:45)

--thirty (--:30) --treinta (--:30) 三十分钟 (--:30

a.m.	a.m.	上午
p.m.	p.m.	下午
What time is it?	¿Qué hora es?	什么时间？
It is one o'clock.	Es la una en punto.	现在一点钟

TIME-RELATED WORDS   PALABRAS RELACIONADOS CON EL TIEMPO 时间相关词汇

a while ago	hace un momento	刚才
all the time	todo el tiempo	始终
always	siempre	总是
date	fecha	日期
day	día	天
day after tomorrow	pasado mañana	后天
day before yesterday	antes de ayer	前天
earlier	mas temprano	初期的
early	temprano	早期的
in a little while	en un pequeño instante	不久
last week	semana pasada	上礼拜
late	tarde	迟的
later	mas tarde	更迟的
midnight	medianoche	午夜
minute	minuto	分钟
month	mes	月
next week	próxima semana	下周
noon	mediodía	中午
occasionally	ocasionalmente	偶而
second	segundo	秒
shortly	enseguida	立刻
sometimes	a veces	有时
soon	pronto	立刻
this afternoon	esta tarde	下午
this evening	esta noche	傍晚
this morning	esta mañana	早晨
this week	esta semana	本周
today	hoy	今天

tomorrow	mañana	明天
tonight	esta noche	今晚
two years ago	hace dos años	两年后
week	semana	周
year	año	年
yesterday	ayer	昨天

BASIC VERBS   VERBOS BÁSICOS   基本动词

to add	agregar	增加
to answer	responder	回答
to arrange	arreglar, organizar	安排
to arrive	llegar	到达
to ask (for)	preguntar	问，要求
to bake	hornear	烤，烘，焙
to bathe	bañar	.沐浴
to be	ser/estar	十
to be able, can	scr apto, poder	能
to begin, start	comenzar	开始
to boil	hervir	沸腾，激动
to break	quebrar, romper	暂停，休息
to bring	traer	停下
to broil	asar	烤；烧
to buy	comprar	购买
to call	llamar	呼叫
to care	cuidar	在意，关心
to carry	llevar	携带，运送
to catch	agarrar	抓住
to change	cambiar	改变
to check	controlar, chequear	检查
to chop	picar	剁碎,砍
to clean	limpiar	打扫
to clear	vaciar, despejar	扫除
to close, shut	cerrar	关闭
to come	venir	来

to communicate	comunicar	交流
to cook	cocinar	烹饪
to count	contar	记数，计算
to cut	cortar	切，剪切
to dance	bailar	跳舞
to describe	describir	描写
to discuss	discutir	讨论
to do	hacer	做
to dress	vestir	穿衣
to drink	beber	喝
to drive	conducir	推动，开车
to dry	secar	干燥
to dust	sacudir, sacarle el polvo	掸掉
to eat	comer	吃
to empty	vaciar	倒空，清空
to end	finalizar, terminar	结束
to enter	ingresar	进入，输入
to exist	existir	存在，生存
to exit	salir	退出
to explain	explicar	解释，说明
to fall	caer	落下
to feel	sentir	触，摸
to fight	pelear, luchar	打架，对抗
to fill (out)	rellenar	充满
to fill (up)	llenar	充满
to find	encontrar	发现
to finish	finalizar	完成
to fire	disparar	点燃，射击
to fix	sujetar, asegurar	固定，确定
to fold	doblar	折叠，包
to follow	seguir	跟随
to fry	freír	油煎
to give	dar	给
to give birth	dar a luz	生孩子
to go	ir	走
to greet	saludar	问候

to guess	adivinar	猜测
to have	tener	有
to heal	curar	治愈
to hear	oír	听见
to help	ayudar	帮助
to hide	esconder	躲,隐藏
to hire	alquilar, contratar	雇用
to hold	sostener	保持
to hurt	herir	受伤
to iron	planchar	熨
to keep	mantener	坚持
to knock	golpear	敲门
to know	conocer, saber	知道
to laugh	reír	笑
to learn	aprender	学习
to leave	dejar	离开
to listen	escuchar	听
to live	vivir	生活
to look	mirar	看
to lose	perder	失去
to love	amar	爱
to make	preparar	产生
to meet	encontrar	会见
to mend	coser, remendar	改善
to mop	limpiar, secar con el trapo	擦洗
to move	mover	移动
to need	necesitar	需要
to open	abrir	开
to operate	operar	操作
to pack	empaquetar, envasar	收拾行李
to pay	pagar	付钱
to peel	pelar	1脱皮
to pick (up)	levantar, recoger	拣(起来)
to play	jugar	玩
to polish	lustrar	磨光
to prefer	preferir	更喜欢

to prepare	preparar	准备
to pull	tirar de	拉
to push	empujar	推
to put	poner	放
to put away	guardar, ahorrar	拿走
to quit	abandonar	停止，退出
to read	leer	读
to receiver	recibir	收到
to recommend	recomendar	推荐
to refill	rellenar	再充填
to remember	recordar	记得
to remove	remover	搬迁
to repair	reparar	修理
to request	pedir	请求
to repeat	repetir	重复
to rest	descansar	休息
to return	regresar	返回
to ride	montar	骑
to rise	subir, elevar	升起
to sauté	saltear	
to say	decir	说
to scrub	fregar	擦净
to seat	tomar asiento	坐位子
to see	ver	看
to select	seleccionar	选择
to sell	vender	卖
to send	enviar	送
to serve	servir	服务
to sew	coser	缝纫
to show	mostrar	出现
to sign	firmar	签名
to sing	cantar	唱歌
to sit	sentar	坐
to sleep	dormir	睡觉
to slice	cortar (en rebanadas)	切
to smell	oler	闻

to spray	pulverizar, rociar	产生水花
to stain	manchar	玷污
to stand	estar (de pie)	站立
to stay	permanecer	逗留, 延缓
to stir	revolver, remover	移动, 传播
to stock	vender	进货采购
to stop	parar, detener	工作
to study	estudiar	学习
to suggest	sugerir	建议, 提出
to sweep	barrer	打扫
to take	tomar	拿走, 取
to talk, speak	hablar	说
to taste	probar, degustar	品尝
to tell	decir	告诉
to think	pensar	认为
to touch	tocar	接触
to try	tratar	尝试
to turn (off)	apagar	转动
to turn (on)	prender, encender	转动
to understand	entender	了解
to use	usar	使用
to vacuum	aspirar	用真空吸尘器打扫
to wait	esperar	等待
to wait (on)	esperar (hasta)	等候
to wake (up)	despertar	醒来
to walk	caminar	步行
to want	querer	想, 想要
to wash	lavar	洗涤
to waste	gastar	浪费
to watch	mirar	观看, 注意
to wave	agitar	示意
to wax	encerar	增大
to wear	tener puesto (ropa)	穿
to wipe	limpiar, pasar un trapo	擦
to work	trabajar	工作
to worry	preocupar	烦恼

to wrap	envolver	覆盖
to write	escribir	写

BASIC ADJECTIVES	**ADJETIVOS BÁSICOS**	基本形容词
aggressive	agresivo	好斗的
ambitious	ambicioso	雄心勃勃
attractive	atractivo	吸引人的
average	medio, promedio	平均的
bad	malo	坏
big	grande	大
bitter	amargo, crudo	痛苦的
bland	soso, desabrido	柔和的
boring	aburrido	令人厌烦的
brave	valiente	勇敢的
bright	brillante	明亮的
broken	roto	碎的
busy	ocupado	忙碌的
challenging	desafiante, retador	挑战性
cheap	barato	便宜的
clean	limpio	干净的
closed	cerrado	关闭的
cold	frío	冷的
comical	cómico	有趣的
convenient	conveniente	方便的
cool	fresco	凉爽的
cooperative	cooperador	合作的
correct	correcto	正确的
cruel	cruel	残酷的
dangerous	peligroso	危险的
delicious	delicioso	可口的
different	diferente	不同的
difficult	difícil	困难的
dirty	sucio	脏的
early	temprano	早的

easy	fácil	容易的
employed	empleado, ocupado	雇用的
energetic	energético	积极的
expensive	caro	昂贵的
extraordinary	extraordinario	非凡的
extroverted	extrovertido	外向性的
fair	justo	公平的
famous	famoso	著名的
far	lejos	遥远的
fast	rápido	快的
fat	gordo	肥胖的
fearful	aterrador	恐怖的
feminine	femenino	女性的
few	varios	很少的
free	libre	自由的
frightening	espantoso	害怕的
funny	divertido	滑稽的
generous	generoso	慷慨的
good	bueno	好的
handsome	apuesto	俊俏的
hardworking	trabajador	苦干的
healthy	saludable	健康
heavy	pesado	沉重的
honest	honesto	诚实的
hot (temperature)	calor	热的
hot (spicy)	picante	热(香)
hungry	hambriento	饥饿的
impatient	impaciente	急躁
imperfect	imperfecto	有缺点
impossible	imposible	不可能
impulsive	impulsivo	有激情
inconvenient	inconveniente	有困难
incorrect	incorrecto	错误的
independent	independiente	独立的
industrious	trabajador	勤勉的
intellectual	intelectual	智力的

intelligent	inteligente	聪明的
interesting	interesante	有趣的
introverted	introvertido	明显的
large	grande	大的
late	tarde	晚的
lazy	holgazán, vago	懒散的
light	liviano	光明的
locked	cerrado	锁定的
loose	suelto, holgado	放松的
loud, noisy	ruidoso	大声,吵闹
many	muchos	许多
masculine	masculino	健壮的
materialistic	materialista	唯物论的
mature	maduro	成熟的
narrow	cerrado	狭窄的
near	cerca	在附近
new	nuevo	新的
old	viejo	旧的，老的
on time	puntual	准时
open	abierto	开放的
opposite	opuesto	相反的
ordinary	ordinario	平常的
organized	organizado	有组织的
patient	paciente	病人的
perfect	perfecto	完美的
pleasant	agradable	舒适的
polite	cortés	礼貌的
pretty	lindo	恰当的
qualified	calificado	有资格的
quick	rápido	快速的
quiet	tranquilo	安静的
responsible	responsable	负责的
right	derecho	恰好的
romantic	romántico	浪漫的
rude	rudo	粗鲁的
safe	salvo	安全的

salty	salado	咸味的
same	mismo	一样的
sensitive	sensible	敏感的
short	corto	短的
sick	enfermo	生病的
sincere	sincero	诚挚的
slow	lento	慢的
small, little	pequeño	小的
sociable	sociable	友好的
soiled	sucio	弄脏的
some	alguno	一些
sore	dolorido	酸的
sore, painful	doloroso	痛苦的
sour	agrio	酸腐的
special	especial	特殊的
strange	extraño	奇怪的
strong	fuerte	强壮的
superstitious	supersticioso	迷信的
sweet	dulce	t香甜的
tall	alto	高的
thick	grueso	厚的
thin	fino	薄的
thirsty	sediento	口渴的
tight	ajustado	紧密的
timid	tímido	羞怯的
ugly	feo	丑的
unemployed	desempleado	失业的
unhealthy	insalubre	病弱的
unpleasant	desagradable	讨厌的
unqualified	descalificado	没限制的
used	usado	使用的
warm	templado	温暖的
whole	entero	整个的
wide	ancho, amplio	宽的
wrong	equivocado	错误的
young	joven	年轻的

PARTS OF THE BODY	PARTES DEL CUERPO	身体部位
abdomen	abdomen	腹部
ankle	tobillo	踝节部
arm	brazo	手臂
armpit	axila	腋窝
back	espalda	背
blood	sangre	血
bone	hueso	骨头
brain	cerebro	大脑
breast	pecho	胸
buttock	nalgas	屁股
calf	pantorrilla	小牛
cheek	mejilla	脸颊
chest	pecho	胸膛
ear	oreja	耳朵
earlobe	nódulo de la oreja	耳垂
elbow	codo	肘
eye, eyeball	ojo	眼睛
eyebrow	ceja	眉毛
eyelash	pestaña	睫毛
eyelid	párpado	眼皮
face	rostro	脸
feces	heces	脸部
finger	dedo	手指
fingernail	uña	指甲
foot	pie	脚
forehead	frente	前额
genitals	genitales	外阴部
hair	cabello	头发
hand	mano	手
head	cabeza	头
heart	corazón	心
heel	talón	脚跟
hip	cadera	臀部
jaw	mandíbula	颚

joint	articulación	关节
kidney	riñón	肾
knee	rodilla	膝
kneecap	rótula	膝盖骨
leg	pierna	腿
lip	labio	嘴唇
liver	hígado	肝脏
lung	pulmón	肺
mouth	boca	嘴
muscle	músculo	肌肉
nail	uña	指甲
neck	cuello	颈
nerve	nervio	神经
nose	nariz	鼻子
nostril	orificio nasal	鼻孔
pelvis	pelvis	骨盆
ribs	costilla	肋骨
saliva	saliva	口水
scalp	cuero cabelludo	头皮
shin	canilla	胫骨
shoulder	hombro	肩膀
skeleton	esqueleto	骨架
skin	piel	皮
skull	cráneo	头骨
spine	columna vertebral	脊骨
stomach	estómago	胃
thigh	muslo	大腿
throat	garganta	喉咙
thumb	pulgar	姆指
toe	dedo gordo del pie	脚趾
toenail	uña del pie	脚趾甲
tongue	lengua	舌头
tooth, teeth	dientes, muelas	牙齿
torso	torso	躯干
urine	orina	尿
voice	voz	声音

waist	cintura	腰
wrist	muñeca	手腕

RELATIONSHIPS

RELATIONSHIPS	**RELACIONES**	关系
acquaintance	conocido	熟人
adopted child	niño adoptado	收养的孩子
adoptive parent	padres adoptivos	养父养母
aunt	tía	姑妈
bachelor, bachelorette	soltero	单身汉, 未婚女子
boyfriend	novio	男朋友
brother	hermano	兄弟
brother-in-law	cuñado	内弟
child	niño	内弟
children	niños	孩子们
close friend	mejor amigo	密友
common law	concubino	普通法律
cousin	primo	表亲
daughter	hija	女儿
divorced	divorciado	离婚
elder	mayor	年长的
engaged	comprometido	已订婚的
ex-wife	ex esposa	前妻
family	familia	家庭
father	padre	父亲
father-in-law	suegro	岳父
fiancé, fiancée	prometido	未婚夫, 未婚妻
foster parent	padre adoptivo	养父母
friend	amigo	朋友
girlfriend	novia, amiga	女友
godchild	ahijado	教子
godfather	padrino	神父
godmother	madrina	教母
godparents	padrinos	名义双亲
grandchild	nieto	孙子

grandfather	abuelo	祖父
grandmother	abuela	祖母
great-aunt	tía abuela	伯祖母
great-grandfather	bisabuelo	伯祖父
great-grandmother	bisabuela	曾祖父
great-uncle	tío abuelo	曾祖母
half-brother	hermanastro	同父异母兄弟, 同母异父兄弟
half-sister	hermanastra	同父异母姐妹, 同母异父姐妹
husband	esposo	丈夫
junior	hijo	晚辈
lover	amante	爱人
married	casado	已婚的
Miss	Señorita	小姐
mother	madre	母亲
mother-in-law	suegra	岳母
Mr.	Señor	先生
Mrs.	Señora	太太
Ms.	Señora	小姐
neighbor	vecino	邻居
nephew	sobrino	外甥
niece	sobrina	甥女
older	mayor	年长的
parent(s)	padres	父母
partner	compañero	搭挡
partner	compañero	搭挡
relative	pariente	亲戚
same sex	mismo sexo	同性
senior	padre	年长, 长辈
separated	separado	个别的
single	soltero	单个的
sister	hermana	姐妹
sister-in-law	cuñada	嫂子
son	hijo	儿子
step-brother	hermanastro	异父兄弟
step-father	padrastro	后爹
step-mother	madrastra	后娘

step-sister	hermanastra	异父姐妹
stranger	desconocido	陌生人
uncle	tío	叔叔
widow, widower	viuda, viuda	寡妇
wife	esposa	妻子
younger	mas joven	年轻人

EMOTIONS

EMOTIONS	EMOCIONES	情感
angry	enojado	生气的
anxious	ansioso	焦急的
ashamed	avergonzado	羞愧的
bored	aburrido	烦人的
bothered	apático	费心 的
burned out	escozor, ardor	费尽心思的
busy	ocupado	忙碌的
calm	calmado	平静的
confused	confundido	糊涂的
content	contento	满足的
curious	curioso	好奇的
desperate	desesperado	失望的
disappointed	decepcionado	绝望的
disgusted	disgustado	厌烦的
distracted	distraído	心烦意乱的
embarrassed	avergonzado	为难的
envious	envidioso	妒忌的
excited	entusiasmado	兴奋的
fed up	harto	喂养的
frightened, scared	aterrado, miedoso	受惊,惊吓
frustrated	frustrado	阻挠
furious	furioso	狂暴
grateful	agradecido	感激的
guilty	culpable	有罪的
happy	feliz	幸福的
homesick	extrañar	思乡病的

hostile	hostil	敌对的
hurt	herido	受伤的
impatient	impaciente	急躁
in a bad mood	con mal humor	坏心情
in a good mood	con buen humor	好心情
in love	enamorado	热爱的
inferior	inferior	自卑的
jealous	celoso	嫉妒
lonely	solitario	孤独的
nervous	nervioso	紧张的
proud	orgulloso	骄傲的
resentful	resentido	愤慨的
restless	inquieto	不安宁
relaxed	tranquilo	放松的
sad	triste	悲伤的
satisfied	satisfecho	满足的
sick	enfermo	生病的
sorry	sentido	抱歉的
stressed	estresado	强调的
tense	tenso	紧张的
tired	cansado	疲倦的
uncomfortable	incómodo	不舒适的
upset	disgustado	不安
worried	preocupado	烦恼

MAJOR HOLIDAYS   FERIADOS MAS IMPORTANTES   主要节日

Chanukah (Jewish, December 8-16)
Chanukah (judío, Diciembre 8-16)
光明节 (犹太, 12月8–16日)

Chinese New Year (Chinese, varies between Jan. 21–Feb. 19)
Año Nuevo Chino (Chino, varía entre el 21 de Enero y 19 de Febrero)
中国新年 (华人, 在1月之间变化)

Christmas (Christian, December 25–federal)

Navidad (Cristiana, Diciembre 25–federal)

圣诞节 (基督, 12月25日联邦)

Cinco de Mayo (Mexican, May 5)

Cinco de Mayo (Mexicano, Mayo 5)

Mayo 节 (墨西哥人, 5月5)

Columbus Day (second Monday in October–federal)

Día de la Raza (segundo Lunes en Octubre–federal)

哥伦布节 (在10月的第二个星期一)

Diwali (Hindu New Year, new moon in December)

Diwali (Año Nuevo Hindú, nueva luna en Diciembre)

印度新年 (印度人新年, 在12月内)

Easter (Christian, a Sunday between March 22–April 25)

Pascuas (Cristiano, un domingo entre el 22 de marzo–25 de abril)

复活节 (基督, 在三月22到四月25日之间)

Election Day (first Tuesday in November)

Día de Elecciones (Primer Martes de Noviembre)

选举日 (在11月内的第一个星期二)

Father's Day (third Sunday in June)

Día del Padre (tercer Domingo de Junio)

父亲节 (在6月份的第3个星期天)

Good Friday (Christian, Friday before Easter)

Viernes Santo (Cristiano, viernes antes de Pascuas)

耶稣受难日 (基督, 在复活节前的星期五)

Halloween (October 31)

Noche de Brujas (Octubre 31)

万圣节前夕 (10月31日)

Independence Day (July 4–federal)

Día de la Independencia (Julio 4–federal)

美国独立日（七月4号）

Kwanzaa (African-American, December 26–January 21)

Kwanzaa (Afro-Americano Diciembre 26–Enero 21)

（非洲-美国，12月21到 一月26日）

Labour Day (first Monday in September–federal)

Día del Trabajo (Primer lunes de Septiembre–federal)

劳动节（在9月第一个星期一）

Martin Luther King Jr. Day (third Monday in January–federal)

Martín Luther King (Tercer Lunes en Enero–federal)

马丁路德金节（在1月的第3个星期一）

Memorial Day (last Monday in May–federal)

Día de Recordatorio a los caídos en la guerra (último Lunes de Mayo–federal)

纪念日（在5月上周一）

Mother's Day (second Sunday in May)

Día de La Madre (segundo Domingo de Mayo)

母亲节（在5月内的第二星期天）

New Year's Day (January 1–federal)

Día de Año Nuevo (Enero 1–federal)

新年（1月1号）

President's Day (third Monday in February–federal)

Día de los Presidentes (tercer Lunes de Febrero–federal)

总统日（在2月的第3个星期一）

Ramadan (Muslim holy month of fasting–Oct.-Nov.)

Ramadan (Mes Musulmán Sagrado de Ayuno Oct.–Nov.)

斋月（穆斯林-10月11月.）

Rosh Hashanah (Jewish New Year, usually in October)

Rosh Hashanah (Año Nuevo Judío usualmente, en Octubre)

犹太新年 (犹太的新年, 通常在10月内)

St. Patrick's Day (Christian, March 17)

Día de San Patricio (Cristiano, Marzo 17)

(克里斯琴, 3月17) (基督徒, 3月17)

Thanksgiving (fourth Thursday in November–federal)

Día de Gracias (Cuarto Jueves de Noviembre–federal)

感恩节 (在11月第四星期四)

Valentine's Day (Christian, February 14)

Día de San Valentín (Cristiano, Febrero 14)

情人节 (2月14号)

Veteran's Day (November 11–federal)

Día del Veterano (Noviembre 11–federal)

老战士节 (11月11号)

Yom Kippur (Jewish holy day, usually in October)

Yom Kippur (Día Sagrado Judío, usualmente en Octubre)

赎罪日 (犹太人的宗教节日, 一般在10月)

Purim (Jewish, 2 days usually in March)

Purim (Judío, 2 días usualmente en Marzo)

普林节 (犹太, 三月的某两天)

Passover (Jewish, 8 days usually in April)

Pascua (Judío, 8 días usualmente en Abril)

逾越节 (犹太, 四月的8天)

COLORS	COLORES	颜色
beige	beige	米黄色

black	negro	黑色
blond, blonde	rubio	金黄色
blue	azul	蓝色
brown	marrón	棕色
brunette	morena	深肤色
clear	claro	明亮的
dark	oscuro	黑色
fair	rubio, blanco	白皙
gold	dorado	金色
green	verde	绿色
grey/gray	gris	灰色
light	claro	明亮
navy	azul marino	海兰色
orange	naranja	橙色
pink	rosa	粉红色
purple	púrpura	紫色
red	rojo	红色
silver	plateado	银色
tan	bronceado	黝黑
white	blanco	白色
yellow	amarillo	黄色

SYMBOLS / SÍMBOLOS / 符号

°F Degree Fahrenheit	°F Grados Fahrenheit	°F华氏度
°C Degree Celsius	°C Grados Celsius	°C 度摄氏
™ trademark	™ Marca Registrada	™ 商标
+ plus, addition sign	+ mas signo de adición	+ 加, 添加症状
- minus, subtraction sign	- menos, signo de sustracción	− 减, 减法症状
x times, multiplication sign	x por, signo de multiplicación	x 时间, 乘号
÷ divided by, division sign	÷ dividido por, signo de división	÷ 划分了由, 除号
= equal, equal sign	= igual, signo igual	
© copyright sign	© derechos de reproducción	© 版权症状
& and, ampersand	& y, ampersand	& 符号
% percent, percentage	% por ciento, porcentaje	% 百分比, 百分比

$ **dollar sign**	$ signo de dólar	$ 美元符号
# **number sign, pound**	# signo de número, libra	# 数字症状, 磅
! **exclamation mark**	! signo de exclamación	! 叹号
? **question mark**	? Signo de interrogación	? 问号
< **less than**	< menos que	< 不到,小于
> **greater than**	> mayor que	> 大于
/ **backslash**	/ barra	/ 反斜杠
" **quotation mark**	" comillas	引语标记
' **apostrophe**	' apóstrofe	' 撇号
( ) **brackets, parentheses**	( ) paréntesis	( ) 括号
, **semi-colon**	, punto y coma	, 分号
: **colon**	: dos puntos	: 冒号
, **comma**	, coma	, 逗点
. **period**	. punto	周期
* **asterisk, star**	* asterisco, estrella	* 星号

WEIGHTS/MEASURES   PESOS/ MEDIDAS   重量/测量

IMPERIAL/AMERICAN	IMPERIAL/ AMERICANO	英制的/美制的
teaspoon	cucharadita	茶匙容量
tablespoon	cucharada	一大汤匙容量
ounce	onza	盎司
cup	taza	杯
pint	pinta	品脱
quart	cuarto de galón	夸脱(容量单位)
gallon	galón	加伦
inch	pulgada	英寸
foot	pie	英尺
yard	yarda	码
mile	milla	英里
gross	bruto	罗（计数单位）
ton	tonelada	吨
truckload	camionada	一货车之量

METRIC	MÉTRICO	米制
centimeter	centímetro	厘米
meter	metro	米
kilomete	kilómetro	公里
gram	gramo	克
kilogram	kilogramo	公斤
tonne	tonelada	公吨
milliliter	mililitro	毫升
litre	litro	公升

MATH TERMS	TÉRMINOS MATEMÁTICOS	数学术语
add	sumar	增加
amount	cantidad	数量
angle	ángulo	角度
average	promedio	平均
balance	balance	平衡
circle	círculo	圆圈
cone	cono	锥形物
corner	ángulo	角落
cube	cubo	立方
curve	curva	曲线
cylinder	cilindro	圆筒, 圆柱体
decimal	decimal	十进制
degree	grado	度
design	diseño	设计
diagonal	diagonal	对角线
divide	dividir	划分, 分开
dozen	docena	一打, 12个
edge	límite, filo	边, 边缘
equation	ecuación	方程
even	igual	偶数, 偶校验
fraction	fracción	分数
half-dozen	media docena	半打, 6个
height	altura	高度

horizontal	horizontal	水平的
length	longitud	长度
level	nivel	水平,水平面
line	línea	行
mark	marca	标记
multiply	multiplicar	多样地
pair	par	对
parallel	paralela	平行
pattern	patrón	模式
percent	porcentaje	百分比
point	coma decimal	点
portion	porción	一分
proportion	proporción	比例
ratio	radio	比率
rectangle	rectángulo	长方形
shape	forma	形状
square	cuadrado	平方
straight	recto	笔直地
subtract	restar	减
sum	sumar	金额
total	total	总量
triangle	triángulo	三角形
uneven	irregular	奇数的
unit	unidad	单位
vertical	vertical	垂直的
width	ancho	宽度

SIGNS	**SIGNOS**	标志
airport	Aeropuerto	机场
Authorized Personnel Only	Sólo Personal Autorizado	闲人勿进
Bus Stop	Parada de colectivo	汽车站
Caution	Cautela	注意
Closed	Cerrado	关门
Corrosive	Corrosivo	腐蚀剂

Crosswalk	Cruce Peatonal	人行横道
Customer Parking	Estacionamiento para Clientes	停车场
Customs	Aduana	海关
Danger	Peligro	危险
Deliveries	Repartos	交货
Detour	Desvío	弯路
Do Not Block Entrance	No Bloquear la Entrada	不许阻塞入口
Do Not Cross	No Cruzar	不许拐弯
Do Not Disturb	No Molestar	别扰乱
Do Not Litter	No arrojar Basura	不要丢东西
Emergency Exit	Salida de Emergencia	紧急情况出口
Entrance	Entrada	入口
Exit	Salida	出口
Fire Escape	Escalera de Incendios	火灾逃生出口
For Rent	En Alquiler	出租
For Sale	En Venta	出售
Handicapped	Discapacitado	残废
Hazardous	Peligroso	冒险
High Voltage	Alto Voltaje	高电压
Hospital	Hospital	医院
Information	Información	信息
Keep Off The Grass	Prohibido pisar el césped	禁止践踏草坪
Keep Out	Prohibido el paso	切勿靠近
Men, Gentlemen	Hombres, Caballeros	男人, 绅士
Next Cashier	Próximo cajero	下一个司库
Next Window Please	Próxima ventana, por favor	请再开下一扇窗户
No Admittance	Prohibida la entrada	禁止进入
No Dogs Allowed	No se permiten perros	禁止人行
No Entrance	Prohibido entrar	没有入口
No Left Turn	Prohibido doblar a la izquierda	禁止左转
No Parking	Prohibido Estacionar	没有停车
No Passing	Prohibido Pasar	不过去
No Right Turn	Prohibido Doblar a la Derecha	禁止右转
No Smoking	Prohibido Fumar	禁止吸烟
No U Turn	Prohibido doblar en U	禁止回转
No Vacancy	Completo	没有空缺

Now Hiring	En Alquiler	现在出租
Occupied	Ocupado	占据
One Way	Mano única	单行道
Open	Abierto	开
Out Of Order	Desordenado	故障中
Parking Lot	Playa de Estacionamiento	停车场
Pedestrian Crossing	Cruce de peatones	行人穿越道
Please Wait To Be Seated	Por favor esperar a ser atendido	行人穿越道
Poison	Veneno	毒物
Pull	Tirar	拉
Push	Empujar	推
Railroad Crossing	Cruce de trenes	交叉的铁路
Ready	Listo	准备好了
Reception	Recepción	接收
Restricted Access	Acceso Restringido	限制的通行
Restroom	Baño	公厕
Shipping and Receiving	Envío y Recepción	发货并且收到
Slow	Lento	减速
Speed Limit	Límite de Velocidad	速度极限
Station	Estación	车站
Stop	Pare	停止
Subway	subterráneo	地铁
Toilet, Restroom	Baño	厕所, 公厕
Tow-Away Zone	Zona donde opera la grúa	拖走地区
Traffic Circle	Círculo Tráfico	交通环形线
Under Construction	En Construcción	修建中
Use Other Door	Use otra puerta	使用另外的门
Vacant/Vacancy	Vacante	空白/空缺
Wait	Espere	等待
Walk	Camine	步行
Welcome	Bienvenido	受欢迎
Wet Floor	Piso Húmedo	湿地板
Wet Paint	Pintura fresca	湿油漆
Women, Ladies	Mujeres, Damas	女人, 女士
Wrong Way	Camino Equivocado	错误的路线
Yield	Ceda el paso	产量

FOOD WORDS: | PALABRAS DE COMIDAS: | 食物

FRUIT	FRUTAS	水果词汇
apple	manzana	苹果
apricots	damasco	杏
avocado	palta	鳄梨
bananas	bananas	香蕉
blackberry	mora	黑莓
blueberry	arándano	蓝莓
canteloupe	melón	罐头
cherry	cereza	樱桃
clementine	clementina	克莱门氏小柑橘
coconut	coco	椰子
fig	higo	无花果
dates	dátil	枣椰子
grapefruit	pomelo	葡萄柚
grapes	uva	葡萄
kiwi	kiwi	几维
lemon	limón	柠檬
lime	lima	酸橙
mango	mango	芒果
orange	naranja	橘子
peach	durazno	桃树
pear	pera	梨
pineapple	ananá	菠萝
plum	ciruela	洋梅
pomegranate	granada	石榴
prunes	pasa de ciruela	梅脯
raisins	pasa de uva	葡萄干
raspberry	frambuesa	悬钩子
strawberry	frutilla	草莓
tangerine	mandarina	柑桔
tomato	tomate	西红柿
watermelon	sandía	西瓜

VEGETABLES	VEGETALES	蔬菜
asparagus	espárrago	芦笋
basil	albahaca	罗勒
bamboo shoots	brotes de bambú	竹笋
bean sprouts	poroto	豆芽
bok choy	bok choy	博克球
broccoli	brócoli	花椰菜
brussel sprouts	repollitos de bruselas	发芽
cabbage	repollo	卷心菜
carrots	zanahorias	胡萝卜
cauliflower	coliflor	花椰菜
celery	apio	芹菜
chili	ají, chile	红辣椒
cilantro	cilantro	胡荽叶
corn	maíz	玉米
corn on the cob	mazorca de maíz	圆状玉米
cucumber	pepino	黄瓜
eggplant	berenjena	茄子
fennel	hinojo	茴香
garlic	ajo	大蒜
gingerroot	galleta de jengibre	姜根
green beans	chaucha	嫩菜豆
green onions	cebolla de verdeo	绿洋葱
green pepper	pimiento verde	绿椒
jalapeños	jalapeños	药喇叭脂
lettuce	lechuga	莴苣
mushrooms	hongos	蘑菇
okra	calalú	秋葵
onions	cebollas	洋葱
parsley	perejil	欧芹
peas	arvejas	豌豆
potatoes	papas	马铃薯
red pepper	pimiento rojo	红辣椒
snowpeas	tirabeque, arveja	豌豆
soybeans	porotos de soja	大豆
spinach	espinaca	菠菜

squash	calabaza, zapallo	南瓜
sweet potato	batata	香甜的马铃薯
turnip	nabo	萝卜
yam	batata	山药
zucchini	zucchini	南瓜

BREAD	**PAN**	面包
baguette	baguette	法国棍子面包
biscuit	bizcocho	饼干
bread	pan	面包
brown	pan negro	棕色
croissant	medialuna	新月形面包
English muffin	rollo de pan que suele ser tostado	英国松饼
French toast	torreja	法国人烤面包
kaiser	panecillo con semillas de amapolas	皇帝
muffin	pan tostado	松饼
pancake	panqueque	薄烤饼
pita	pan árabe	皮塔饼
roll, bun	pancito	转动,甜面包
rye	pan de centeno	黑麦
toast	tostada	干杯
tortilla	tortilla	玉米粉圆饼
waffle	waffle	华大饼干
white	pan blanco	蛋白
whole wheat	pan integral	小麦

DAIRY PRODUCTS	**PRODUCTOS LACTEOS**	奶制品
butter	manteca	黄油
cheese	queso	干酪
cream	crema	乳脂
cream cheese	queso cremoso	奶油干酪
eggs	huevos	鸡蛋
ice cream	helado	冰淇淋
margarine	margarina	代黄油
milk	leche	牛奶
sour cream	crema	酸腐的乳脂

yogurt	yogurt	酵母乳
MEAT	**CARNE**	肉
bacon	panceta	咸肉
beef	bife	牛肉
bone	hueso	骨头
breast	pechuga	胸肉
chicken	pollo	鸡肉
chop	costilla	砍
clam	almeja	蚌
crab	cangrejo	螃蟹
duck	pato	鸭
filet	filete	肉片,鱼片
fillet	filete	鱼片
fish	pescado	鱼
game	caza	野味的
ham	jamón	火腿
hamburger	hamburguesa	汉堡包
lamb	cordero	羔羊
leg	pata	腿
lobster	langosta	龙虾
oysters	ostra	牡蛎
pork	puerco	猪肉
rabbit	conejo	野兔
rack	costillar	烧酒
ribs	costilla	肋骨
roast	asado	烤制品
salmon	salmón	大马哈鱼
sashimi	sashimi	生鱼片
sausage	salsa	香肠
scallops	concha de vieira	扇贝
shellfish	marisco	甲壳
shrimp	camarón	虾
sirloin	carne molida	牛腰肉
steak	churrasco	牛排
sushi	sushi	寿司,生鱼片冷饭团

tenderloin	lomo	牛腰部嫩肉
tuna	atún	鲔鱼
turkey	pavo	火鸡
veal	ternera	小牛

DESSERT/SNACKS	**POSTRES/PICADAS**	甜菜/快餐
cake	torta	蛋糕
candy	caramelo	糖果
cheesecake	tarta de queso	酪饼
chips	papas fritas	筹码
chocolate	chocolate	巧克力
cookie	galletitas dulces	小甜饼
cracker	galletitas de agua	脆饼
crisp	papa frita	碎皮
crumble	postre de fruta	面包屑
flan	flan	果馅饼
ice cream	helado	冰淇淋
nuts	nueces	坚果
pastry	pastelito	面粉糕饼
pie	pastelito	馅饼
popcorn	pochoclo, palomitas de maíz	爆米花
pretzel	galleta salada	法国皮撒
pudding	budín	布丁
shortcake	tarta de fruta	油酥糕饼
sorbet	helado de agua	果汁冰糕
sundae	sundae	圣代
tart	tarta	果馅饼
tiramisu	tiramisu	蒂朗

DRY GOODS	**COMESTIBLES NO PERECEDEROS**	干燥的货物
baby food	comida de bebé	婴儿食品
beans	poroto	豆子
bouillon	caldo	肉汤
brown sugar	azúcar negra	棕色的糖

canned food	conserva	罐装的食物
cereal	cereal	谷物
chicken broth	caldo de pollo	鸡肉汤
chocolate	chocolate	巧克力
coffee	café	咖啡
condiments	condimentos	佐料
corn syrup	jarabe de maíz	玉米果汁
cornstarch	maizena	玉蜀黍淀粉
couscous	cuscús	蒸肉丸
flour	harina	面粉
granola bars	barra de cereales	酒吧
hoisin sauce	hoisin sauce	hoisin 酱汁
lard	grasa de cerdo	猪油
maple syrup	jarabe de arce	枫树果汁
mayonnaise	mayonesa	蛋黄酱
miso paste	miso paste	浆糊
molasses	melaza	糖蜜
mustard	mostaza	芥末
olive oil	aceite de oliva	橄榄油
oyster sauce	salsa de ostras	牡蛎酱汁
pasta	pasta	意大利面制品, 意大利面食
peanut butter	manteca de maní	花生黄油
pepper	pimienta	辣椒
pickle	pickles	淹菜
rice	arroz	大米
rice vinegar	vinagre de arroz	大米醋
salad dressing	preparación de ensalada	穿衣的色拉
salsa	salsa	沙拉
salt	sal	食盐
sesame oil	aceite de sésamo	芝麻油
shortening	mantequilla	缩短
soy sauce	salsa de soja	酱油
spaghetti	tallarines	绝缘套管
spices	especias	香料
sugar	azúcar	糖
tea	té	茶

vanilla	vainilla	香子兰
vinegar	vinagre	醋
wild rice	arroz silvestre	野大米

OTHER FOOD WORDS — OTRAS PALABRAS DE COMIDAS — 另外的食物词汇

bitter	amargo	痛苦
canned	enlatado	罐装
cold	frío	冷淡的
condiment	condimentos	佐料
digestive	digestivo	消化
fat	con grasa	脂肪
fresh	fresco	新鲜
frozen	congelado	结冰
grease	grasa de cerdo	脂肪
grain	grano	谷物
hot	caliente	辣的
mixed	mezclado	混合
sour	agrio	酸腐
spice, spicy	picante	香料, 香
sweet, sweets	dulce, dulces	香甜, 糖果
vitamin	vitamina	维生素
warm	caliente	温暖

HOUSEHOLD PRODUCTS — PRODUCTOS DOMÉSTICOS — 家庭产品

aluminum foil	papel de aluminio	铝陪衬
alcohol	alcohol	白酒
battery	pilas	电池
bleach	lejía, lavandina	变白
cigarette	cigarrillo	香烟
comb	peine	梳子
conditioner	acondicionador	调节器
dental floss	seda dental	牙科的乱丝
deodorant, anti-perspirant	desodorante, antitranspirante	除臭, 止汗药

detergent	detergente	去垢
diapers	pañal	尿布
diaper cream	crema para pañales	尿布乳脂
fabric softener	suavizante	织品变柔软
feminine hygiene	higiene femenina	女性的卫生
hairbrush	cepillo para el cabello	发刷
laundry detergent	jabón para lavar la ropa	去垢的洗衣店
light bulb	bombilla para la luz	灯泡
lotion	loción	液
magazine	revista	杂志
napkins, serviettes	servilletas	小块布或毛巾,餐巾
newspaper	diario	报纸
paper towel	toallitas de papel	论文毛巾
plastic wrap	bolsa de plástico de envolver	塑料包
plastic bag	bolsa de plástico	塑料袋
razor, razor blade	máquina de afeitar	剃刀,剃刀片
sandwich bags	bolsas para sándwich	三明治袋子
sanitary pads	tabletas sanitarias	洁净的垫
shampoo	champú	洗发精
soap	sopa	肥皂
stain remover	removedor de manchas	污点搬运工
tampons	tampones	棉球
tape	cinta	磁带
tissues	pañuelo de papel	织物
toilet bowl cleaner	limpia inodoros	更干净的厕所碗
toilet paper	papel higiénico	厕所纸
toothpaste	pasta de dientes	牙膏
waxed paper	papel encerado, parafina	给纸上蜡
window cleaner	limpiavidrios	窗户清洁剂

AROUND THE HOUSE   SOBRE LA CASA   在房子附近

air conditioner	aire acondicionado	空调
alarm clock	despertador	闹钟
alley	camino, sendero	胡同

apartment	departamento	公寓
ashtray	cenicero	烟灰缸
attic	ático	顶楼
backyard	patio trasero	后院
balcony	balcón	阳台
barbeque	parillada	烤肉架
basement	sótano	地下室
bathroom/restroom	baño	洗澡间/厕所/公厕
bathtub	bañadera	澡盆
bed	cama	床
bedroom	habitación	卧房
bedspread	cubrecama	床单
blanket	frazada	毯子
blender	licuadora	no translation
blinds	persiana	窗帘
bookcase	biblioteca	书架
broom	escoba	扫把
building	edificio	大楼
candle	vela	蜡烛
carpet	alfombra	地毯
ceiling	techo	天花板
chair	silla	椅子
closet	armario	洗手间
coffee maker	maquina de café	咖啡制造者
coffee table	mesa ratona	咖啡桌子
condominium	condominio	共管
corner	esquina	角落
crib	cuna	童床
curtain	cortina	门帘
deck	suelo	甲板
décor, decoration	decoración	英国管, 装饰
deep fryer	freidora	深油煎
desk	escritorio	桌子
dining room	comedor	进餐的房间
dishwasher	lavaplatos	洗碗机
door	puerta	门

dresser	vestidor	梳装台
driveway	camino que lleva a una casa	车道
dryer	secadora	更干燥
dustpan	pala	簸箕
DVD player	reproductor de DVD	数字激光视盘播放器
electric heater	estufa eléctrica	电的加热器
elevator	ascensor	升降机
entrance	entrada	入口
exit	salida	出口
family room, rec room		
habitación familiar, habitación de recreación		家庭房间, 娱乐场房间
fence	cerco	篱笆
fireplace	hogar	壁炉
frame	marco	结构
freezer	freezer	冰箱
frying pan	freidora	油煎平底锅
garden	jardín	花园
gate	puerta	大门
grill	parrilla	烤架
hair dryer	secador de cabello	更干燥的头发
hall, hallway	vestíbulo, hall	大厅, 门厅
hand mixer	batidora de mano	手混合器
hose	manguera	长筒袜
iron, ironing board	plancha, tabla de planchar	铁, 熨董事会
kitchen	cocina	厨房
lamp	lámpara	灯
laundry room	lavadero	洗衣店房间
lawn mower	máquina de cortar el césped	草坪
living room	living	客厅
lot	lote, terreno	许多
mailbox	buzón	邮箱
mattress	colchón	空气垫
microwave	microondas	微波
mirror	espejo	镜子
neighborhood	barrio	邻居
oven	horno	炉

painting	cuadro, pintura	着色
patio	patio trasero	天井
picture	foto	图片
pillow	almohada	枕垫
pillowcase	funda de la almohada	枕头套
placemat	mantel individual	布置
porch	porche	走廊
radio	radio	无线电
rag	trapo	破布
ramp	rampa	斜坡
refrigerator	refrigerador	冰箱
rice cooker	olla para arroz	大米炊具
rug	alfombra	地毯
screen	pantalla	屏幕
sheet	sábana	表格
shower	ducha	淋浴
sidewalk	vereda	人行道
sink	lavaplatos	水池
sofa/couch	sofá	沙发/睡椅
stairs	escaleras	楼梯
stereo	stereo	立体声
stove	cocina	炉
swimming pool	piscina	泳池
telephone	teléfono	电话
television	televisión	电视
toaster	tostadora	祝酒人
towel	toalla	毛巾
townhouse	casa de la ciudad	市政厅
vacuum cleaner	aspiradora	真空吸尘器
vase	florero	瓶
VCR	videograbadora	录像机
washcloth	toallita	面巾
washer, washing machine	lavarropas	洗,洗衣机
water heater	calefón	水加热器
window	ventana	窗户
wood stove	horno a leña	木头炉

KITCHEN ITEMS	ÍTEMS DE COCINA	厨房条款
bowl	bol	碗
broom	escoba	扫把
can opener	abrelatas	能更开
cheese grater	rallador de queso	干酪刺激
chopsticks	palillos chinos	筷子
cloth	repasador	布
colander, strainer	colador	滤锅
corkscrew	sacacorchos	开塞钻
cup, mug	taza	杯, 大杯
cutlery	cuchillería	刀剑
cutting board	tabla de cortar	切董事会
dish, dishes	plato, platos	盘子, 盘子
dustpan	pala	簸箕
fire extinguisher	extinguidor de incendios	灭火器
fork	tenedor	叉形物
frying pan	sartén	油煎锅
garbage	basura	垃圾, 废物
garbage can	tacho de basura	垃圾能
glass	vaso	玻璃
kettle	pava	水壶
knife	cuchillo	小刀
mop	mopa	擦洗
plate	plato	板
pot	olla	壶
rag	trapo	破布
rubber gloves	guantes de goma	橡胶手套
salad bowl	bol de ensalada	色拉碗
scissors	tijeras	剪刀
scrub brush	cepillo de fregar	擦净刷子
sponge	esponja	海绵体
spoon	cuchara	汤勺
timer	temporizador de horno	定时器
towel	toalla	毛巾
trash can, garbage	tacho de basura	垃圾能, 垃圾

tray	bandeja	盘子
utensil	utensilio	器皿
wok	wok	炒菜锅

CLOTHING/APPAREL   ROPA   衣服/衣服

accessory	accesorio	附加物
apron	delantal	围裙
belt	cinturón	皮带
blouse	blusa	罩衫
boot	bota	靴子
boxer shorts	boxers	拳击手短裤
bra, brassiere	corpiño	奶罩, 胸罩
bracelet	brazalete	手镯
briefcase	cinturón	公文包
briefs	calzoncillos	摘要
button	botón	钮扣
camisole	camisola	女背心
cap	gorra	帽子
chain	cadena	链
coat	saco	大衣
collar	collar	领子
dress	vestido	衣服
earplugs	tapones para oídos	耳栓
earring	aros	耳环
flip flop	chancleta	拈扑通落下
full-length	largo	全身
gloves	guantes	手套
goggles	gafas	护目镜
gown	vestido	长袍
hair net	redecilla	头发卡
handbag	cartera	手袋
handkerchief	pañuelo de mano	手绢
hard hat	casco	防护帽
hat	sombrero	帽子
helmet	casco	头盔

hem, hemline	dobladillo	缝，底边
high heels	tacos altos	高跟鞋
hosiery	calcetería	针织衣物
inseam	entrepierna	内接缝
jacket	chaqueta	夹克衫
jeans	jeans	牛仔裤
jewelry	joyería	珠宝
knapsack	mochila	背囊
knee high	hasta la rodilla	高膝
lingerie	lencería	女内衣
long-sleeved	manga larga	长袖
make-up	maquillaje	化妆
mask	máscara	面具
mittens	mitón	露指手套
necklace	collar	项链
nightgown	camisón	女睡衣
nylons	medias de nylon	尼龙
overalls	overol	外套
overcoat	sobretodo	外衣
pajamas	pijamas	睡衣
pants	pantalón	裤子
panty hose	pantimedias, bombachas	裤袜
panty, panties	braga	内裤，短裤
purse	monedero	钱包
raincoat	piloto	雨披
ring	anillo	响
robe	bata	长袍
running shoe	zapatillas	跑鞋
safety glasses	gafa de seguridad	安全眼镜
sandal	sandalia	凉鞋
scarf	bufanda	围巾
shirt	camisa	衬衫
shoe, shoes	zapato, zapatos	鞋子，鞋子
shorts	shorts, pantalón corto	短裤
short-sleeved	mangas cortas	短袖运动衫
skirt	pollera	裙子

slacks	pantalones	懒散
sleeve	mangas	套袖
sleeveless	sin mangas	无袖
slip	calzoncillo	滑倒
sneaker	zapatillas	运动鞋
sock, socks	soquete, medias	短袜, 短袜
steel-toe boots	botas con punta de acero	钢脚趾靴子
stocking	media	长袜
strap, strapless	bretel, sin bretel	皮带
suit	traje	套装
sunglasses	lentes de sol	墨镜
sweater	sweater	毛衣
sweatpants	pantalón de gimnasia	汗裤
sweatshirt	sudadera	汗衫
swimsuit	malla, traje de baño	游泳衣
tank top	camiseta sin mangas, chaleco	背心
thong	tanga	皮带
tie	corbata	系住
t-shirt	remera	衬衫
tuxedo	esmoquin	无尾礼服
umbrella	paraguas	伞
undergarment	prenda interior	贴身衣
undershirt	camiseta	贴身内衣
underwear	ropa interior	衬衣
uniform	uniforme	制服
vest	chaleco	汗衫
wallet	billetera	钱包
watch	reloj	手表
zipper	cierre	拉链

SHOPPING	**DE COMPRAS**	购物

May I help you?

¿En que puedo ayudarlo?   我可以帮助你吗？

I am looking for -.   Estoy buscando-.   我正在寻找-.
I need a -.   Necesito un -.   我需要一-.

What size do you wear/take?
       ¿Qué talle usa?   你穿/拿什么尺寸?

Small (S)   Pequeño (S)   小
Medium (M)   Medio (M)   媒介
Large (L)   Grande (G)   大
Extra Large (XL) Extra Grande (XL)   特大(
I'm not sure.   No estoy seguro.   我不肯定.

This is too big/small.
       Esto es demasiado chico/grande.   这是太大/小.

It's too tight/loose.
       Es demasiado ajustado/suelto.   它太紧/松.

It fits/ doesn't fit.
       Esto me queda bien/no me queda bien.   它适合/ 不合适的.

I don't like the color.
       No me gusta el color.   我不喜欢颜色.

Would you like to try it on?
       ¿Le gustaría probárselo?   你想试用它在上吗?

I would like to try this on.
       Me gustaría probármelo.   我想试用这在上.

Where are the fitting rooms?
       ¿Dónde esta el probador?   适合的房间在哪儿?

Can I bring you another size/color?
       ¿Puedo traerle en otro color/talle?   我能带给你另外的尺寸/颜色吗?

Do you have this in another size?

    ¿Tiene este en otro talle?   你有另外的尺寸吗？

How did you make out?   ¿Cómo lo confeccionó?   你怎么辨认呢？

I will take this one.   Me llevaré esta.   我要这个.

Is it on sale?   ¿Está en venta?   它是出售的吗？

We are having a sale right now.

    Estamos teniendo una liquidación en este momento.

                          现在我们正在举办展销.

Do you like this one?   ¿Le gusta este?   你喜欢这个吗？

How will you be paying?   ¿Cómo lo pagará?   你想怎样付钱？

We don't take personal checks.

    No aceptamos cheques.   我们不接受个人支票.

How much is it?   ¿Cuánto cuesta?   它要多少钱？

Is the tax included?   ¿Está incluido el impuesto?   包括税是吗？

It is hand wash/dry clean only.

    Solo puede ser lavado a mano.   它是仅仅手洗/干燥.

I'd like to return this.

    Me gustaría devolver esto.   我想退回这个.

Which one do you like?   ¿Cuál le gusta?   你喜欢哪个？

Which one do you prefer?

    ¿Cuál prefiere?   你更喜欢哪个？

How many would you like?

    ¿Cuántos le gustarían?   你想要多少？

We no longer have those in stock.
No tenemos mas esos en stock.　　　　　　我们不再有那些存货.

We can order more.
Podemos pedir mas.　　　　　　.我们能订更多的.

Those are on back-order.
Esos están pedidos.　　那些是订货的.

How did you hear about us?
¿Cómo se enteró de nosotros?　　　你是怎么听说我们的？

Something else?
¿Algo más?　　　　　　有的别的东西？

Will that be all?
¿Alguna otra cosa?　　　　　那是全部该多好？

Will there be anything else today?
¿Algo más habrá hoy?　　　　今天会有其他东西吗？

AT A RESTAURANT	EN UN RESTAURANTE	在一个餐馆
aperitif	aperitivo	开胃酒
appetizer	aperitivo, tapa	开胃酒
ashtray	cenicero	烟灰缸
banquet	banquete	宴会
bar	bar	酒吧
beer	cerveza	啤酒
beverage	bebida	饮料
bowl	bol	碗
bread	pan	面包
bread basket	canasta de pan	面包篮子
bread plate	plato de pan	面包板
breakfast	desayuno	早餐

brunch
    combinación de desayuno y almuerzo   早午餐

buffet	buffet	餐台

bus person
    persona que transporta elementos a la mesa   乘务员

butter knife	cuchillo para la manteca	黄油小刀
cash	efectivo	现金
cashier	cajero	出纳
casual	casual	随便
champagne	champagne	香槟
check, bill	cheque	票, 帐单
chef	chef	厨师
china	china	陶瓷
clear the table	limpiar la mesa	清洗桌子
cocktail	cocktail	鸡尾酒
coffee	café	咖啡
coffee cup	taza de café	咖啡杯
condiments	condimentos	佐料
cook	cocinar	煮
course (first course)	plato (primer plato)	路线(第一球场)
cream	crema	乳脂
credit card	tarjeta de crédito	信用卡
cup	taza de café	杯
customer	cliente	顾客
debit	débito	借方
decaffeinated	descafeinado	脱去咖啡因
dessert	postre	餐后甜点
dining room	salón comedor	进餐的房间
dinner	cena	晚饭
dish	plato	盘子
draft	minuta	草稿
drink	beber	喝
elegant	elegante	端庄
entrée	plato principal	入场许可
family	familia	家庭
flatware	cubertería	扁平餐具

food allergy	alergia a la comida	食物过敏症
fork	tenedor	叉形物
gin	ginebra	陷阱
glass	vaso	玻璃
glassware	cristalería	玻璃器皿
guest	invitado	客人
high chair	silla alta	高级的椅子
hors d'oeuvre	entrada, primer plato	no translation
hostess, host	anfitriona/anfitrión	女主人，主人
ice bucket	hielera	冰桶
ice cube	cubo de hielo	冰立方
iced	helado	冰冷的
iced tea	te helado	茶
juice	jugo	果汁
kitchen	cocina	厨房
knife	cuchillo	小刀
large	grande	大
lemonade	limonada	柠檬水
liqueur	licor	烈酒
liquor	bebidas alcohólicas fuertes	白酒
lounge	salón	休息室
low-carbohydrate	bajo en carbohidratos	低糖类
low-fat	bajo en grasas	低脂肪
low-sodium	bajo en sodio	低钠
lunch	almuerzo	午餐
martini	martini	马丁尼酒
medium	medio	媒介
menu	menú	菜单
mineral water	agua mineral	矿泉水
napkin	servilleta	小块布或毛巾
non-alcoholic	sin alcohol	非酒精性
non-smoking	área de no fumadores	非吸烟
noodles	fideos	笨蛋
on the rocks	con hielo	在摇上
on the side	de una parte	在边上
pasta	pasta	干面食

pepper	pimienta	辣椒
pepper grinder	molinillo de pimienta	辣椒
plate	plato	板
platter	fuente	唱片
price	precio	价格
rare	raro	稀罕
reservation	reservación	保留
restroom	baño	公厕
rice	arroz	大米
rum	ron	糖酒
salad	ensalada	色拉
salad dressing	aliño para ensalada	穿衣的色拉
salt	salón	食盐
saucer	salsa	盘子
scotch	escocés	苏格兰威士忌
seafood	mariscos	海产食品
section	sección	节
server	servir	服务者
serving	porción	服务
shaken	agitar	摇晃
shift	turno	移动
side order	orden	边顺序
silverware	platería	银器
small	pequeño	小
smoking section	sección de fumadores	吸烟的节
snack	refrigerio	快餐
soft drink	refresco	软饮料
soup	sopa	汤
soup bowl	bol de sopa	汤碗
soup spoon	cuchara para sopa	汤汤勺
sous chef	sous chef	厨师
sparkling	espumoso, con gas	发火星
special	especial	特殊
spoon	cuchara para sopa	汤勺
steak knife	cuchillo para carnes	牛排小刀
stirred	agitado	搅动

straight up	arreglado	笔直地起来
tablecloth	mantel	桌布
take the order	tomar el pedido	拿订单
tea	té	茶
teacup	taza de té	茶杯
teaspoon	cucharita de té	茶匙
tip, gratuity	propina	末端, 小帐
tray	bandeja	盘子
vegetable	vegetal	蔬菜
vegetarian	vegetariano	食草动物
vodka	vodka	伏特加
waiter, waitress	mozo, moza	侍者, 女服务员
water	agua mineral	水
well-done	bien cocido	熟透
whiskey	whisky	威士忌
wine glass	vaso de vino	葡萄酒玻璃
wine list	lista de vinos	葡萄酒列表
wine-red	vino tinto	葡萄酒-红
wine-white	vino blanco	葡萄酒-白

I'd like to make a reservation.

Me gustaría realizar una reserva.　　　　喜欢做预定.

Do you have a reservation?

¿Tiene una reserva?　　　　你举办预定吗？

Table for _____?

¿Mesa para _____?　　　　桌子为_____?

For how many people?

¿Para cuántas personas?　　　　为多少人？

For what time?

¿Para qué hora?　　　　为什么时间？

May I have your name?

¿Me podría decir su nombre?　　　　　　　　我可以有你的名字吗？

Is there a phone number where we can reach you?

¿Me podría dar un número de teléfono donde la pueda encontrar?

在那里我们能联系你的一个电话号码吗？

Party of (number)

Fiesta de (número)　　　　　　　　　　　党的 (数字)

Would you like smoking or non-smoking?

¿Le gustaría en el área de fumadores o en la de no fumadores?

你将喜欢吸烟或非吸烟吗？

This is a non-smoking restaurant.

Este es un restaurante donde no se puede fumar.

这是一个非吸烟的餐馆.

May I see a menu?

¿Puedo ver el menú?　　　　　　　　　　我可以看见菜单吗？

May I take your order?

¿Puedo tomar su pedido?　　　　　　　　我可以拿你的订单吗？

Are you ready to order?

¿Esta listo para ordenar?　　　　　　　　你准备好了订？

Have you decided yet?

¿Ya se ha decidido?　　　　　　　　　　已经你已经决定吗？

What is the special of the day?

¿Cuál es la especialidad de hoy?　　　　什么是特殊今日？

Today's special is -.

La especialidad de hoy es -.　　　　　　今天的特殊是-.

I would like the _____.
> Me gustaría la _____.　　　　　　　　我将喜欢_____.

May I have the _____.
> Puedo tener el _____.　　　　　　　　可能我有-.

Do you have - ?
> ¿Tiene -.?　　　　　　　　你有- ?

Does it come with -?
> ¿Viene con-?　　　　　　　　它来与-?

Is everything alright?
> ¿Esta todo bien?　　　　　　　　任何事物是好的吗?

Sorry to keep you waiting.
> Discúlpeme que lo hice esperar.　　　　　　抱歉让你等待.

Is there_____in that dish?
> Tiene _____ ese plato?　　　　　　在那里_____在那个盘子中?

Do you have any food allergies?
> ¿Tiene alguna alergia a la comida?　　　你有任何食物过敏症吗?

I am allergic to _____.
> Soy alérgico a _____.　　　　　　我是患过敏症的_____.

Is it very spicy?
> ¿Es muy picante?　　　　　　它是很香的吗?

Would you like rice or potatoes?
> ¿Qué le gustaría arroz o papas?　　　你将喜欢大米或马铃薯吗?

Would you like soup or salad?
> ¿Qué le gustaría sopa o ensalada?　　　你将喜欢汤或色拉吗?

How would you like your steak done?
¿Cómo le gusta el bife cocido?　　　　你将怎么喜欢做的牛排？

How would you likc that cooked?
¿Cómo le gustaría eso horneado?　　　怎么将你那样地煮了？

Baked, mashed or fried?
¿Horneado, molido o frito?　　　　　烘过，捣碎或油煎吗？

May I have some water please?
¿Me puede traer agua?　　　　　　　可能我一些请已经流水？

Can we get some more (bread)?
¿Me podría traer mas pan?　　　　　我们能得到一些更多的(面包)吗？

Is there meat in that?
¿Tiene carne eso?　　　　　　　　　在那里肉在那吗？

This food is cold.
Esta comida esta fría.　　　　　　　这食物是冷的.

Can you please heat this up?
¿Me lo podría calentar?　　　　　　你能请加热这起来吗？

I am on a special diet.
Yo hago una dieta especial.　　　　我在一份特殊的食谱上.

Can I bring you anything else?
¿Puedo traerles algo más?　　　　　我能带给你其他东西吗？

Would you like to see a dessert menu?
¿Le gustaría ver el menú de postres?　你想看见甜菜菜单吗？

Would you like tea or coffee?
¿Qué le gustaría te o café?　　　　　你将喜欢茶或咖啡吗？

How will you be paying?

¿Cómo pagará? 你将怎么付钱?

Please bring me the bill.

Por favor, tráigame la cuenta. 请带给我帐单.

Can we have separate checks?

¿Puede traernos cuantas separadas? 我们能核对一下分开的吗?

Can we get a doggy bag?

¿Puede traernos una bolsa para el perro? 我们能得到一个狗袋子吗?

Can I wrap this up for you?

¿puedo envolver esto por Ud? 为你我能包这起来吗?

Please come again.

Por favor vuelvan. 请再来.

FAST FOOD	COMIDA RÁPIDA	快餐
all-you-can-eat	todo lo que pueda comer	随便吃
bagel	bollo con forma de rosquilla	圈饼
baked	horneado	烘过
breaded	empanada	涂面包屑后烹制
bun	bollo, panecillo	甜面包
burrito	burrito	墨西哥玉米煎饼
cappuccino	capuchino	热牛奶咖啡
char-broiled	asado al carbón	焙字符
cheeseburger	hamburguesa con queso	三明治
condiment bar	barra de condimento	佐料酒吧
creamer	jarrita para crema	盛乳皮的盆
croissant	medialuna	新月形面包
croissant	medialuna	新月形面包
deep-fried	frito con abundante aceite	深油煎

disposabled	esechable	可任意使用
donut	rosquilla	油炸圈饼
eat-in	comer en casa	在吃
espresso	expresso	蒸馏咖啡
fish and chips	pescado y papas fritas	鱼和炸薯条
french fries	papas fritas	french油煎
fried	frío	油煎
fried chicken	pollo frito	油煎了鸡肉
grease	grasa	脂肪
grilled	hecho en la parrilla, asado	烤
hamburger	hamburguesa	汉堡包
hashbrown	papas y cebollas doradas en la sartén	大麻
heat lamp	papa caliente	加热灯
hot dog	pancho	热狗
ice cream machine	máquina de helado	冰淇淋机
ice machine	máquina de hielo	冰箱
iced milk	helado hecho con leche descremada	牛奶
ketchup	ketchup	蕃茄酱
latte	Café latte	薄片
lid	tapa	盖
microwave	microondas	微波
milkshake	malteada, licuado con leche	奶昔
muffin	bollo de pan que suele servirse tostado	松饼
mustard	mostaza	芥末
nuts	nueces	坚果
onion rings	aros de cebolla	洋葱圈
oven	horno	炉
paper cups	tazas de papel	纸杯
pie	tarta	馅饼
pizza	pizza	比萨
pizza box	caja de pizza	比萨盒子
refill	rellenar	再充填
relish	guarnición, salsa	意味
rotisserie	rotiseria	烤肉店
sandwich	sándwich	三明治
sandwich box	caja de sándwich	三明治盒子

sauce	salsa	酱汁
self-serve	autoservicio	自助服务
shake machine	licuadora	搅拌机
shake mix	Mezcla batida	搅拌
soda, pop	soda, gaseosa	苏打水
soft serve	refresco	柔软的发球
sprinkles	espolvoreado	喷撒
storeroom	almacén	库房
styrofoam	espuma de polyestireno	发泡苯乙稀
sub, submarine	submarino	附属，海底的
sugar	azúcar	糖
suggestive sell	venta sugestiva	暗示出售
super size	tamaño súper	超大尺寸
syrup	almíbar	果汁
taco	taco	玉米面豆卷
take out	para llevar	外带
timer	cronómetro del horno, microondas 定时器	
to go	ir	走
toppings	cobertura	顶层加料
tray	bandeja	盘子
treat	gusto (de darse un gusto)	对待
two-for-one	dos por uno	两个为一个
utensils	utensilios	器皿
vat	cuba	大缸
wrap	envoltorio	包
wrapper	envoltorio	书皮

Is that for here or to go?
 ¿Es para aquí o hay que ir?   是想待在这里或离开？

Will you be eating in?
 ¿Comerán allí en su casa?   你正在吃吗？

Would you like a tray?
 ¿Le gustaría una bandeja?   你想来一盘吗？

What size would you like?
¡qué tamaño Ud. Prefiere?   你喜欢什么尺寸？

What would you like on that?
¿Qué le gustaría ponerle a eso?   你喜欢它什么？

Would you like fries with that?
¿Le gustaría acompañarlo con papas fritas?   你想油煎它吗？

Would you care for a salad?
¿Quisiera una ensalada?   你想要一盘色拉吗？

That will be ____.
Eso sería-.   那将是_____.

Please drive through.
Por Favor diríjase.   请开车通过.

Would you care for dessert?
¿Le gustaría un postre?   你喜欢甜菜吗？

Can I take your order?
¿Puedo tomar su pedido?   我能为你喜下订单吗？

It will take a few minutes for your order.
Me tomará algunos minutos su pedido.   你的订单将花几分钟.

I'll bring it to your table.
Se lo traigo a su mesa.   我会把它放到你的桌子的.

I'm sorry we don't serve that here.
Discúlpeme pero no servimos eso aquí.   我抱歉的我们不提供这服务.

I'm sorry we don't take credit cards.
Discúlpeme pero no aceptamos tarjetas de crédito.
我抱歉我们不接受信用卡.

Welcome to _____.
> Bienvenido a _____.

欢迎光临 _____.

Have a nice day.
> Que tengan un buen día.

祝你愉快.

Thanks, come again.
> Gracias, espero que vuelvan.

感谢, 再来.

The restrooms are around the corner.
> Los baños están a la vuelta de la esquina.

公厕在拐角处.

SERVER/BUSSING INSTRUCTIONS   INSTRUCCIONES PARA MESEROS   服务/商业说明

Please arrive ___ minutes before your shift.
> Por favor lleguen___minutos antes.

请在你的移动 的分钟内到达.

You must wear clean and pressed black pants/skirt and a white shirt.
> Debe usar pantalones/pollera negros limpios y una camisa blanca.

你必须穿干净并且黑的裤子/裙子和一件白衬衫.

Set the tables with glassware, silverware and napkins.
> Acomode la mesa con cristalería, platería y servilletas.

在桌子放置玻璃器皿, 银器和小块布或毛巾.

Greet guests with a smile.
> Salude a los clientes con una sonrisa.

笑迎顾客.

Remove extra table settings.
> Quitar los elementos no necesarios de la mesa.

拿开额外的桌子物品.

Bring bread, water and butter to the table.
> Traer pan, agua y manteca a la mesa.

带面包, 水和黄油 放到桌子.

Refill the water glasses often.
Servir frecuentemente los vasos con agua.
经常杯子上水.

Carry silverware and glasses on a tray.
Cargar la platería y vasos en una bandeja.
用一个盘子放上银器和杯子带走.

Don't touch the rim of the glass.
No tocar el borde de los vasos.
不要触摸杯子的边缘.

Handle silverware by the stem only.
Tome la platería solo por el pie.
只使用银制品.

Remove empty plates promptly.
Levantar los platos vacíos de la mesa rápidamente.
迅速地移开空板.

Use a tray to carry food and dishes.
Usar una bandeja para llevar la comida y los platos.
使用一个盘子带食物和盘子.

Prepare the service area.
Preparar el área de servicio.
准备服务区.

Restock the service area.
Cargar el stock en el área de servicio.
重新进货服务区.

Prepare coffee, hot water and ice water.
Preparar café, agua caliente y agua fría.
煮沸咖啡, 热水和冰水.

Refill condiment containers.
Rellenar los contenedores de condimentos.
再充填佐料集装箱.

Clean service stations.
Limpiar las estaciones de servicio.　　　　打扫加油站.

Replace soiled tablecloths with clean ones.
Remplazar los manteles sucios por limpios.
用干净的代替弄脏的桌布.

Fold the napkins.
Doblar las servilletas　　　　　　　　折叠小块布或毛巾.

Fill the bread basket.
Llenar las paneras.　　　　　　　　　装满面包篮子.

Clear the table.
Limpiar la mesa.　　　　　　　　　清洗桌子.

Empty the ashtrays.
Vaciar los ceniceros.　　　　　　　空烟灰缸.

SANITATION RULES　　　　REGLAS SANITARIAS　　　卫生规则

Keep hands and fingernails clean at all times.
Mantenga las manos y uñas limpias siempre.
所有时间保持手和指甲干净卫生.

Always use soap and hot water.
Usar siempre jabón y agua caliente.　　　]总是使用肥皂和热水.

Wash your hands after eating and using the washroom.
Lavar las manos después de comer y luego de ir al baño.
在吃房和使用厕所后请洗你的手.

Wash your hands after handling meat, poultry or seafood.

Lave sus manos luego de tocar carne, pollo o calamares.

在接触了肉，家禽或海产食品以后洗你的手.

There is no smoking on the job.

No fumar en el trabajo.   不能在工作上吸烟.

You must keep your hair tied back or covered.

Mantener el pelo atado o cubierto.   你应该把头发系住或盘起.

Do not cough, sneeze or spit near food.

No toser, estornudar o escupir cerca de la comida.

别做咳嗽，喷嚏，或吐食物.

Do not come to work with a contagious illness.

No venir al trabajo con una enfermedad contagiosa.

有传染的病请不要工作.

Your uniform must be clean.

Su uniforme debe estar limpio.   你必须保持制服的干净.

Wash all fruit and vegetables.

Lavar todas las frutas y vegetales.   清洗所有的水果和蔬菜.

Keep all food covered when possible.

Mantener toda la comida cubierta cuando es posible.

尽可能遮盖隔离所有的食物.

Keep fresh food refrigerated.

Mantener la comida fresca refrigerada.   保持新鲜的食物清凉.

Always use clean utensils and cookware.

Siempre usar limpios los utensilios y elementos de cocina.

总使用干净的器皿和炊具.

Use clean water for washing.

Utilizar agua limpia para lavar.　　　　　　　使用干净的水进行清洗.

Use the proper amount of detergent.

Utilizar la cantidad apropiada de detergente.
使用正确数量清洗剂去垢.

Rinse utensils with clean water in a different sink.

Enjugar los utensilios con agua limpia en un diferente lavaplatos.
使用干净的水在不同的水池冲洗器皿.

Handle clean dishes with clean hands or gloves.

Tomar los platos limpios con las manos limpias o guantes.
用干净的手或手套处理干净的盘子.

Do not towel-dry dishes.

No secar los platos con repasador.　　　　　不用毛巾擦干燥的盘子

Wrap the food well.

Envolver bien la comida.　　　　　　　　　很好地包裹食品.

Disinfect the counter/table/sink.

Desinfectar la mesada/mesa/lavaplatos.
给柜台/桌子消毒/下沉.

AT A HOTEL	EN EL HOTEL	在宾馆
adjoining rooms	cuartos contiguos	连接的房间
air-conditioning	aire acondicionado	空气调节
availability	disponibilidad	可用性
babysitting service	servicio de cuidado de niños	服务
balcony	balcón	阳台
bar	bar	酒吧
barber	peluquero	理发员
bathtub	inodoro	澡盆

bedspread	cubrecama	床单
bellman, bell attendant	botones	鸣钟者, 铃值班员
bible	Biblia	圣经
blanket	frazada	毯子
breakfast	desayuno	早餐
buffet	buffet	餐台
business district	distrito de negocios	企业区域
cable television	televisión por cable	有线电视
carpet	alfombra	地毯
check in	registrarse	办理登记手续
check out	irse	结帐
cleaning cart	carrito de limpieza	清扫大车
clock radio	radio reloj	收音机闹钟
coat hanger	perchero de abrigos	衣架
coffee maker	máquina de café	咖啡壶
comb	peine	梳子
concert	concierto	音乐会
concierge	conserje	看门人
conference room	sala de conferencias	会议房间
continental breakfast	desayuno continental	欧陆式早餐
corridor	corredor	走廊
cot	catre	简易窄床
crib	cuna	童床
curtains, drapes	cortinas	门帘, 窗帘
dataport	puerto de datos	no translation
deadbolt	cerradura	锁扭
desk clerk	recepcionista	桌子职员
dining room	salón comedor	进餐的房间
directory	directorio	目录
disco	disco	迪斯科
discount	descuento	折扣
Do Not Disturb	No Molestar	别扰乱
door	puerta	门
double bed	cama doble	双人床
double room	habitación doble	两人间
drawer	cajón	抽屉

elevator	ascensor	升降机
exercise room	habitación de ejercicio	锻练房间
express checkout	registrar la salida expresa	表达结帐
extra towels	toallas extras	额外的毛巾
fan	ventilador	扇子
fax machine	aparato para fax	传真机器
fitness room	habitación para entrenar	适当性房间
floor	piso	地板
fold-out couch	sofá plegable	折页睡椅
front desk	escritorio frontal	前面的桌子
furniture	muebles	家具
gallery	galería	画廊
gift shop	negocio de regalos, regalería	礼品商店
guest	huésped	客人
gym, health club	club de gimnasia	体育馆, 健康俱乐部
hair dryer	secador de pelo	更干燥的头发
hairdresser	peluquería	理发师
hallway	entrada	门厅
heater	calefactor	加热器
hiking trail	excursiones	远足旅行
honeymoon suite	suite de luna de miel	蜜月家具
hot tub, Jacuzzi	jacuzzi	热浴盆
housekeeping	mucama	家务
ice	hielo	冰
ice bucket	cubeta de hielo	冰桶
ice machine	maquina de hielo	冰箱
indoor pool	pileta bajo techo	户内水池
Internet hook-up	Internet banda ancha	因特网连接
iron	plancha	铁
ironing board	tabla de planchar	熨衣板
jogging trail	sendero para jogging	轻推痕迹
key	llave	钥匙
key card (card key)	llave de auto	关键的卡片(卡片钥匙)
king-size bed	cama de tamaño enorme	大号的床
kitchenette	kitchenette	小厨房
lamp	lámpara	灯

laundry room	lavandería	洗衣店房间
light	luz	光
light bulb	bombilla de luz	灯泡
linens	trapos	麻布
lobby	vestíbulo	大厅
local attractions	atracciones locales	本地的吸引力
local calls	llamadas locales	本地电话
lock	cerradura	锁
long distance calls	llamadas de larga distancia	长途电话
luggage rack	portaequipajes	行李架
luggage, bags	equipaje	行李
manager	manager	经理
map	mapa, plano	地图
massage	masaje	按摩
mattress	colchón	空气垫
mattress pad	almohada	空气垫
message	mensaje	消息
mini-bar	mini-bar	袖珍型酒吧
mirror	espejo	镜子
museum	museo	博物馆
newspaper	diario	报纸
night manager	manager/gerente en la noche	晚上经理
nightclub	club nocturno	夜总会
nightstand	lugar nocturno	床头几
no vacancy	completo, cupo agotado	没有空缺
noise	ruido	噪音
outdoor pool	pileta en el exterior	室外水池
park	parque	公园
pay-per-view movies	películas pague-por-ver	电影
pay phone	teléfono público	公用电话
pets	mascotas	宠物
photocopier	fotocopiadora	影印
pillow	almohada	枕垫
place of worship	lugar de culto	礼拜的地点
queen-size bed	cama enorme	大号的床
quiet hours	horas tranquilas	安静的小时

ramp	vía de acceso	斜坡
rate	nivel	比率
refrigerator	refrigerador, heladera	冰箱
rental	alquiler	租借
reservation	reservación	保留
restaurant	restaurante	餐馆
room	habitación	空间
room service	habitación de servicio	客房服务员
safe	seguro	安全
service	servicio	服务
sewing kit	kit para coser	缝纫工具包
shampoo	shampoo	洗发精
sheets	sábanas	表格
shopping district	área de compras	购物区
shopping mall	mercado de compras	商业网点
shower	ducha	淋浴
shower cap	gorra de baño	淋浴帽
shower curtain	cortina de baño	淋浴门帘
shuttle (bus)	servicio de enlace	梭(公共汽车)
sight-seeing	visita a lugares de interés	观光
single bed	cama simple	单身床
single room	habitación simple	单个的房间
sink	lavaplatos	水池
sitting area	living	坐的区域
soap	jabón	肥皂
spa	spa	矿泉
sports	deportes	运动
stairs	escaleras	楼梯
stationery	artículos de papelería	信纸
suitcase	maleta	提箱
suite	suite de luna de miel	整套
supplies	suministros	供应
swimming pool	piscina	泳池
tennis court	cancha de tenis	网球场
theatre	teatro	剧院
thermostat	termostato	自动调温器

tip, gratuity	propina	末端, 小帐
tissues	pañuelos de papel	织物
toilet	toallas	厕所
toilet paper	toallas de papel	厕所纸
toiletries	artículos de tocador	化妆品
toothbrush	cepillo de dientes	牙刷
toothpaste	pasta de dientes	牙膏
tour	tour, excursión	旅行
vacancy	vacante	空缺
valuables	objetos de valor	贵重物品
VCR	Videograbadora	录像机
vending machine	máquina expendedora	贩卖的机器
view	vista	看法
wake-up call	llamada para levantarse	醒来-打电话起来
wheelchair	silla de ruedas	轮椅
window	ventana	窗户

How may I help you?
¿Cómo puedo ayudarle?   我可以怎么帮助你?

Do you have a room?
¿Tiene una habitación?   你有一间房间吗?

I'm sorry, we're full.
Discúlpeme, pero esta lleno.   抱歉的, 我们, 回答完整.

I'd like to make a reservation, please.
Me gustaría hacer una reserva.   喜欢做预定, 请.

For what date(s)?
¿Par qué fecha?   为注明日期的?

For how many nights?
¿Por cuántas noches?   为多少晚上?

How long will you be staying?
¿Cuánto durará su estadía?   你将呆在多长?

For how many guests?

¿Para cuántos huéspedes?   为多少客人？

For one person.

Para una persona.   为一个人．

For two people.

Para dos personas.   为2个人．

For two adults and two children.

Para dos adultos y dos niños.   为2个成人和2个孩子．

What is your best rate?

¿Cuál es su mejor nivel?   你的最好的比率是什么？

Is breakfast included?

¿El desayuno esta incluido?   包括的早餐是吗？

Do you have a handicapped-accessible room?

¿tiene una habitación accesible para discapacitados?

你有一间残废的可靠近的房间吗？

Do you allow pets?

¿Permiten mascotas?   你允许宠物吗？

I'm sorry, we don't allow pets.

Discúlpeme, pero no permitimos mascotas.

抱歉的，我们穿上，允许宠物．

What is the rate?

¿Cuál es el precio?   比率是什么？

The rate is_____ per night.

El precio es __ por noche.   比率是 ____ 每晚上．

Will you be arriving late?
  ¿Llegaran tarde?   你将晚到达吗？

I will be arriving late.
  Llegare tarde.   我将晚到达.

Would you like to guarantee your reservation?
  ¿Le gustaría asegurar la reserva?   你想保证你的保留吗？

I will need a credit card.
  Necesitare una tarjeta de crédito.   我想要一张信用卡.

Which credit card will you be using?
  ¿Cuál tarjeta de crédito usará?   你将使用哪个信用卡？

What is the number?
  ¿Cuál es el número?   数字是什么？

What is the expire/expiration date?
  ¿Cuál es la fecha de vencimiento?   终结/呼出日期是什么？

I would like a double room.
  Me gustaría una habitación doble.   我将喜欢两人间.

I would like a king-size bed.
  Me gustaría una cama king-size.   我将喜欢一张大号的床.

I would like a non-smoking room.
  Me gustaría una habitación en un área de no fumadores.
  我将喜欢一间非吸烟的房间.

I would like to be on the _____ floor.
  Me gustaría estar en el _____ piso.   我想在上 ____ 地板.

Do you have a swimming pool?
  ¿Tiene pileta de natación?   你有一个泳池吗？

Do you have a gym/fitness room?

¿Tiene una habitación de ejercicio?　　　你有一间体育馆/适当性房间吗？

Do you have an airport shuttle?

¿Tiene servicio de enlace al aeropuerto?　你有一个机场梭吗？

What time does the restaurant stop serving?

¿A qué hora termina el restaurante de servir?　餐馆什么时间停止服务？

May I have a wake-up call?

¿Me podría despertar con un llamado por teléfono?

我可以有一醒来-打电话起来吗？

For what time?

¿Para que hora?　　　　　　　为什么时间？

Here is your key.

Aquí esta su llave.　　　　　这是你的钥匙.

This is the key to the mini-bar.

Esta es la llave del mini bar.　　这是到袖珍型酒吧的钥匙.

All calls will be charged to your room.

Todas las llamadas serán cargadas en su habitación.

所有的呼叫将被控告到你的房间.

Please charge that to my room.

Por favor cargue esto a mi habitación.　请收费到我的房间.

Would you like help with your bags/luggage?

¿Le puedo ayudar con sus maletas/equipaje?

与你的袋子/行李你将喜欢帮助吗？

I will have your bags sent up.

Tendré sus maletas enviadas.　　　我将把你的袋子被送了起来.

I hope everything was satisfactory.
 Espero que todo haya sido satisfactorio. 我希望任何事物是圆满的.

May I have some extra towels?
 ¿Me puede dar mas toallas? 我可以有一些额外的毛巾吗?

I'll have that sent to your room.
 Enviaré eso a su habitación. 有送了到你的房间.

How late is ____ open?
 ¿Hasta qué hora esta abierto? 怎么样晚 ____ 开?

I'd like to order room service.
 Me gustaría ordenar el servicio de habitación. 想订客房.

Do I have any messages?
 ¿Tengo algún mensaje? 我有任何消息吗?

Checkout is at _____.
 Para retirar se del hotel es a _____. 结帐在_____.

Check-in is at _____.
Registrarse es a _____. 登记在_____.

Your room is ready.
 Su habitación esta lista. 你的房间是准备好了的.

Your room is not ready yet.
 Su habitación todavía no esta lista. 你的房间仍然没有准备好了的.

They are making up your room.
 Están preparando su habitación. 他们正在打扫你的房间.

Please make up the room.
 Por favor prepárenme la habitación. 请打扫房间.

Can you tell me how to get to _____.
¿Me puede decir como llegar a _____?　　能你告诉我怎么到达_____.

I'd like to check out.
Me gustaría irme.　　我想核对一下.

Did you enjoy your stay?
¿Disfruto de su estadía?　　你享受停留吗?

I hope you enjoyed your stay.
Espero que haya disfrutado su estadía.　　我希望你享受了停留.

I'd like to speak with the manager.
Me gustaría hablar con el gerente.　　我想与经理一起说话.

Please bring my luggage down.
Por favor bajeme el equipaje.　　请带我的行李在下面.

Can you please arrange a taxi?
¿Puede llamar a un taxi?　　你能请安排一辆出租车吗?

Where do I catch the shuttle?
¿Dónde tomo el servicio de enlace?　　我在哪儿找到梭子?

One moment, please.
Un momento, por favor.　　请稍等片刻.

HOUSEKEEPING INSTRUCTIONS　INSTRUCCIONES PARA EL SERVICIO DE LIMPIEZA 家务说明

Adjust the heating or air-conditioning to the proper level.
Ajustar el calefactor o el aire acondicionado al nivel apropiado.
调配加热或到合适的水平的空调.

Check that the T.V. and radio are working.
Controlar que la T.V. y radio estén funcionando.
检查T.V无线电正在工作.

Clean the bathroom.

Limpiar el baño.   打扫洗澡间.

Clean the windows and mirrors.

Limpiar espejos y ventanas.   打扫窗户和镜子.

Complete your daily report.

Completar su reporte diario.   完成你的每日的报告.

Do not knock if there is a "Do Not Disturb" sign.

No golpear si hay un cartel que dice "No molestar."
如果有一个" 不要扰乱" 标志, 不要敲门

Dust the furniture.

Sacudir los muebles.   尘土家具.

Empty the garbage can.

Vaciar el cesto de la basura.   空垃圾能.

If there is no answer, enter the room and leave the door open.

Si no hay respuesta, entrar a la habitación y deje la puerta abierta.
如果没有回答, 进入房间请离开.

Knock on the door and announce, "Housekeeping."

Golpear la puerta y anunciar "Servicio de Limpieza."
敲门并且宣布, "客房部."

Lock the door when you leave.

Cerrar la puerta cuando sale.   当你离开时锁门.

Make a final check before you leave.

Hacer un control final antes de salir.   在你离开以前做一次最终的检查.

Make the bed with clean linen.

Hacer la cama con sábanas limpias.   用干净的麻布铺床.

Mop the floor.
Pasar el trapo al suelo.   擦洗地板.

Notify the supervisor if something is damaged or missing.
Notificar al supervisor si algo esta dañado o perdido.
如果一些东西被损坏，那么通报监督人或失去.

Open the curtains.
Abrir las ventanas.   打开门帘.

Place soiled linen in your laundry bag.
Poner las sábanas sucias en la bolsa de lavandería.
把弄脏的麻布放置在你的洗衣店袋子里.

Polish the furniture.
Encerar los muebles.   波兰式家具.

Replace the desk supplies.
Remplazar los suministros del escritorio.   代替桌子供应.

Replenish the bathroom supplies.
Reponer los suministros del baño.   补充洗澡间供应.

Report any items a guest has left behind.
Informar sobre cualquier ítem que el huésped haya dejado.
报导一位客人任何条款在最后.

Restock the cart with supplies.
Reponer el carro con suministros.   用供应重新进货车.

Scrub the floor.
Fregar el piso.   擦净地板.

Strip the bedding.
Quitar la ropa de cama.   脱去固定.

Sweep the floor.
Barrer el piso.   打扫地板.

Turn down the thermostat.
Bajar el termostato.   关闭自动调温器.

Turn off the lights.
Apagar las luces.   关掉灯.

Vacuum the room/hallway/carpet.
Aspirar la habitación/vestíbulo/alfombra.
空间房间/门厅/地毯.

Vacuum under the bed.
Aspirar debajo de la cama.   在床下面的空间.

Wax the floor.
Encerar el piso.   给地板上蜡于.

Wear gloves when cleaning the bathroom.
Usar guantes cuando limpia el baño.   当打扫洗澡间时穿手套.

MAINTENANCE	MANTENIMIENTO	维护
adjust	ajustar	调配
air-conditioning	aire acondicionado	空调
algae	alga	水藻
asphalt	asfalto	柏油
assemble	ensamblar	集合
attach	sujetar	属于
axle	eje	心棒
bearing	demora	适合于
belt	cinto	皮带
bent	curva	弯屈
blade	pala	片

blower	calefactor	吹风机
board	tabla	木板
boiler	caldera	锅炉
branch	tubería	分支
brick	ladrillo	砖
broken	roto	碎
broom	escoba	扫把
brush	cepillo	刷子
bush	arbusto, matorrales	矮树丛
cable	cable	电缆线
calibrate	calibrar	校对
carbon dioxide	dióxido de carbono	二氧化碳
carbon monoxide	monóxido de carbono	碳一氧化物
carpenter	carpintero	木匠
carpet	alfombra	地毯
caution	cautela	注意
cement	cemento	接合剂
chain saw	motosierra	链锯
check	controlar	饭馆的帐单
chemincals	productos químicos	化学
chipped	astilla	碎裂
chlorine	cloro	氯气
clog, clogged	atascado	阻塞, 阻塞
cockroach	cucaracha	蟑螂
coil	bobina	卷
compressor	compresor	压缩机
concrete	hormigón	具体
condensation	condensación	浓缩
condenser	condensador	精简
connect	conectar	联接
control	controlar	控制
copper sulfate	sulfato de cobre	铜硫酸盐
cord	cuerda	绳索
courtyard	patio	庭院
cracked	con gritas	裂开
curtain	cortina	门帘

cut	cortar	切
damaged	dañado	损坏
deactivate	desactivar	解除
defective	defectuoso	有缺陷
dig	cavar	挖
dirty	sucio	脏
ditch	zanja	壕沟
dolly	plataforma	娃娃
door	puerta	门
drain	tuberías de desagüe	排水管
drainage	desagüe	排水
duct	conducto	管
eavestrough	alero	no translation
electric	eléctrico	电
electricity	electricidad	电
emergency lighting	luz de emergencia	灯光的紧急情况
enamel	esmalte	瓷釉
engineering	ingeniería	no translation
equipment	equipo	设备
erosion	erosión	腐蚀
evaporator	evaporador	蒸发器
exit	salida	出口
fan	ventilador	扇子
faucet	llave, canilla	水龙头
fence	cerca, valla	篱笆
fertilize	fertilizar	使丰饶
fertilizer	ferlitizante	化肥
filter	filtro	过滤器
fire detector	detector de fuego	火察觉者
fire extinguisher	extinguidor de fuego	灭火器
float	flotador	漂浮
flower	flor	花
fluorescent light	luz fluorescente	荧光灯的光
fluorescent tube	tubo fluorescente	荧光灯的试管
fountain	fuente	源泉
freezer	freezer	冰箱

furniture	muebles	家具
fuse	fusible	保险丝
garbage disposal	triturador de basura	垃圾处置
garden	jardín	花园
gardener	jardinero	园丁
gas	gas	气体
gloves	guantes	手套
grain	grano	谷物
grass	césped	草
gravel	arena gruesa	石子
grease trap	trampilla para grasa	脂肪陷井
grind	trabajo pesado	磨擦
gutter	canaleta	沟
hammer	martillo	榔头
hand	mano	手
heat	calor	热
heating	calefacción	加热
heavy	pesado	沉重
hedge	cercar	篱笆
herbicide	herbicida	除草剂
hinge	bisagra	绞链
hoe	azada	锄地
hole	agujero	洞
hose	manguera	长筒袜
insect	insecto	昆虫
insecticide	insecticida	杀虫药剂
knob	perilla	旋钮
ladder	escalera de mano	梯子
latch	pasador	门闩
lawn	césped	草坪
lawn mower	máquina de cortar el césped	草坪
leaf	hoja	叶
leak	gotear	漏缝
leaking	gotera	渗漏
lever	gotera	杆
light bulb	bombita de luz	灯泡

light plate	placa de luz	轻板
light switch	interruptor de luz	轻开关
lime	cal	石灰
liquid	líquido	液体
load	carga	负担
lock	cerradura	锁
locker room	vestuario	衣帽间
loose	suelto	放松
lubricate	lubricar	润滑
measure	medir	测量
mix	mezclar	混合
motor	motor	马达
mouse	ratón	no trasnslation
mousetrap	ratonera	捕鼠器
mow (the lawn)	cortar el césped	修剪(草坪)
nail	clavar	钉子
nozzle	pico	嘴
nut	tuerca	no trasnslation
oil	aceite	油
out of order	fuera de orden	故障中
out of service	fuera de servicio	从服务
paint	pintura	油漆
panel	pancl	面板
part	parte	部分
pest control	control de plagas	no trasnslation
pesticide	pesticida	杀虫剂
pipe	tubo	管子
plant	planta	植物
plaster	yeso	灰泥
pliers	pinza, alicate	钳子
plumber	plomero	管道工
plumbing	cañerías	管道工程
poisonous	veneno	有害
potable water	agua potable	饮料水
powder	polvo	火药
pressure	presión	压力

pressure gauge	indicador de presión	压力计量
preventive maintenance	mantenimiento preventivo	防护的保持
prune	podar	no translation
pulley	polea	滑轮
pump	bomba	泵
rake	rastrillo	耙子
rat	rata	老鼠
refrigeration	refrigeración	冷却
repair	reparar	修理
replace	remplazar	代替
restricted	restringido	限制
rodent	roedor	啮齿类动物
root	raíz	根
rototiller	motocultor	旋耕机
rotten	sucio	腐烂
rubber boots	botas de gomas	橡胶靴子
rubber gloves	guantes de goma	橡胶手套
sand	arena	沙
saw	sierra	看
screen	pantalla	屏幕
screw	tornillo	螺丝钉
screwdriver	atornillador	螺丝刀
seed	semilla	种子
shingle	paca	木瓦
short circuit	cortocircuito	短路
shovel	pala	铲
shower	regadera	淋浴
shrub	arbusto	灌木
shut-off valve	válvula de cierre	栓汽门
sink	fregadero	水池
smoke detector	detector de humo	烟察觉者
soil	tierra	土壤
spare	repuestos, refacciones	业余
spray	pulverizar	水花
sprinkler	válvula	喷撒
stone	piedra	石头

storeroom	almacén	库房
swimming pool	pileta de natación	泳池
tank	depósito, tanque	坦克
temperature	temperatura	温度
tennis court	cancha de tenis	网球场
thermostat	termostato	自动调温器
tight	apretado, estrecho	紧密
tile	baldosa	瓦
toilet	baño	厕所
tool	herramienta	工具
toolbox	caja de herramientas	工具箱
transplant	transplantar	移种
trash	basura	垃圾
trash can	tarro de basura	垃圾能
trash compactor	compactador de basura	垃圾压土机
tree	árbol	树
trench	zanja	沟渠
tune	sintonizar	调子
twisted	retorcido	no translation
unload	descargar	卸货
vacuum	pasar la aspiradora	空间
valve	válvula	汽门
varnish	barniz	亮漆
voltage	voltaje	电压
walk-in freezer	Cámara freezer	竞选胜利冰箱
wall	pared	墙
wallpaper	papel para empapelar paredes	壁纸
waste	residuo	废物
waste water	agua residual	废物水
weed	yuyo, maleza	杂草
weld	soldar	熔接
wheelbarrow	carretilla	独轮手推车
wire	alambre	电线
wood	madera	木头
work order	orden de trabajo	工作顺序

Here is the gas shut-off valve.

Aquí esta la válvula de cierre del gas.　　这是气体栓汽门.

This is the main electricity switch.

Este es el principal interruptor de electricidad.
这是主要的电开关.

That is the electrical panel.

Eso es el panel eléctrico.　　那是电面板.

Can you change the air-conditioning filters?

¿Puede cambiar los filtros de aire acondicionado?
你能改变空气调节的过滤器吗？

The fans and fan motors must be cleaned and lubricated.

Los ventiladores y los ventiladores de motores deben estar limpios y
lubricados.
扇子和扇子马达必须被清扫并且润滑.

The drain is clogged.

El desagüe está obstruido.　　排水管被阻塞.

Repair the cord on this vacuum cleaner.

Reparar la cuerda en esta aspiradora.　　修理在更干净的这空间上的绳索.

Replace the switchplate in Room 202.

Cambiar la placa del interruptor en la Habitación 202.
在第202间代替.

Please return the tools to the storeroom.

Por favor devolver las herramientas al depósito.
请放回工具至库房.

This door needs a new hinge.

Esta puerta necesita una nueva bisagra.　　这扇门需要一条新绞链.

This window does not open properly.

Esta ventana no abra correctamente.　　　.这扇窗户做不开适当.

Replace the missing tiles in the bathroom.

Por favor cambiar los azulejos en el baño.　在洗澡间代替失去的瓦.

Check all emergency exit lights.

Controlar todas las luces de emergencia de las salidas.

检查所有的紧急情况出口灯.

Replace the batteries in the smoke detectors.

Remplazar las baterías en los detectores de humo.

在烟察觉者代替电池.

Fix the garbage disposal.

Reparar el contenedor de basura.　　　　修理垃圾处置.

Vacuum the swimming pool.

Limpiar con la aspiradora a pileta de natación.

.空间泳池.

Test the water with the chemical kit.

Pruebe el agua con el equipo químico.　　测试有化学的工具包的水.

Keep the temperature at seventy-five degrees.

Mantener la temperatura a setenta y cinco grados.

.在70点坚持温度-5度.

When spraying insecticides, wear a mask.

Usar mascara cuando pulveriza con insecticida.

当喷洒杀虫药剂时, 戴一副面具.

The shrubs should be trimmed to three-feet high.

Los arbustos deben ser podados a tres pies de altura.

灌木应该被整修到高的3只脚.

Prune the branches from those trees.

Podar las ramas de esos árboles.　　　　　从那些树修剪树枝.

Paint the fence around the tennis courts.

Pintar la cerca alrededor de la cancha de tenis.
在网球法庭附近油漆篱笆.

Keep the public areas in working condition.

Mantener las áreas públicas en buen funcionamiento.
把公共的区域放在工作的条件.

Please do a safety check around the property.

Por favor hacer un control de seguridad alrededor de la propiedad.
在财产附近请做安全支票.

Plant the flowers in the beds.

Plantar las flores en el vivero.　　　　　在床中种花.

Rake the leaves.

Rastrillar las hojas.　　　　　　　　　.耙子叶子.

Water the grass.

Regar el césped.　　　　　　　　　　水草.

Add chlorine to the pool.

Agregar cloro a la pileta.　　　　　　把氯气加到水池.

Collect the towels from the locker room.

Recoger los trapos del vestuario.　　　从衣帽间收集毛巾.

Adjust the heater.

Ajustar la calefacción.　　　　　　　调配加热器.

Change the lock.

Cambiar la cerradura.　　　　　　　变化锁.

OFFICE ITEMS	ELEMENTOS DE OFICINA	办公室条款
adding machine	máquina de sumar	增加的机器
air conditioner	aire acondicionado	空调
authorized area	área autorizada	批准的区域
answering machine	contestadora	回答的机器
badge	insignia	证章
basement	sótano	地下室
battery	batería	电池
beeper	beeper	机
binder	carpeta	文件夹
blinds	la ventana da sombra	窗帘
book	libro	书
bookshelf	estantes de libros	书架
briefcase	portafolio	公文包
bulletin	boletín, aviso	告示
cabinet	gaveta	内阁
cafeteria	cafetería	自助食堂
calculator	calculadora	计算器
calendar	calendario	日历
call	llamada	打电话
camera	cámara	照相机
car	auto	小汽车
card	tarjeta	卡片
cargo	carga	货物
cartridge	cartuchera	子弹
cash register	caja registradora	收款机
chair	silla	椅子
clock	reloj	钟
coffee maker	máquina de café	咖啡制造者
computer	computadora	计算机
copier	copiadora	复印机
copy	copiar	拷贝
correspondence	correspondencia	通信
database	base de datos	数据库
desk	escritorio	桌子

desktop (computer)	escritorio	桌面 (计算机)
dictionary	diccionario	字典
DVD (digital video disk)	reproductor de DVD	数字激光视盘 (数字的视频磁盘)
disk	disco	磁盘
drawer	cajón	抽屉
drive	disco	开车
electrical cable	cable eléctrico	电的电缆线
elevator	ascensor	升降机
e-mail	e-mail	电子邮件
employee entrance	entrada de empleados	雇员入口
entrance	entrada de empleados	入口
envelope	sobre	信封
equipment	equipo	设备
eraser	goma	橡皮
escalator	escalera mecánica	自动扶梯
exit	salida	出口
extension (phone)	extensión telefónica	扩展(电话)
extension cord	cable de extensión	扩展绳索
fan	ventilador	扇子
fax (facsimile)	fax	传真(传真)
file folder	archivador	文件文件夹
filing cabinet	gaveta	走的内阁
front counter	mostrador frontal	前面的柜台
front desk	escritorio frontal	前面的桌子
garage	garaje	车库
hardware	hardware	硬件
hallway	pasillo	门厅
headset	auriculares	耳机
hole punch	perforadora	洞穿孔机
ink	tinta	墨水
intercom	intercomunicador	内部通信系统
keyboard	teclado	键盘
label	rótulo	标签
lamination	laminación	层压
laptop	portátil	膝上计算机
light	luz	光

lobby	hall	大厅
locker	cerradura	衣柜
mail	mail	邮件
marker	marcador	标记
memo (memorandum)	memo, memorando	备忘录 (便笺)
message	mensaje	消息
microwave	microondas	微波
monitor	monitor	监视
mouse	mouse, ratón	老鼠
name tag	etiqueta de identificación	名字标签
notebook	cuaderno	笔记本
office	oficina	办公室
outlet	toma de corriente	出口
page	página	页
pager	beeper	传呼机
paper	papel	纸
paper clip	clip de papel	论文片断
paper shredder	trituradora de papel	论文切碎机
parking	estacionar	停车
parking lot	estacionamiento	停车场
pay phone	teléfono público	公用电话
pen	lapicera	钢笔
pencil	lápiz	铅笔
photocopier, Xerox	fotocopiadora, Xerox	影印, 施乐
plant	plantar	植物
postage	franqueo	邮费
printer	impresora	印刷工
program	programa	节目
projector	proyector	投影机
public telephone	teléfono público	公共的电话
radio	radio	无线电
reception desk	escritorio de recepción	服务台
restroom	baño	公厕
room	habitación	空间
ruler	regla	统治者
scanner	scanner	扫描仪

scissors	tijeras	剪刀
screen	pantalla	屏幕
security alarm	alarma de seguridad	安全警报
security code	código de seguridad	安全代码
shelf	estante	架子
sign-in (sheet)	registro de entrada	症状-在 (表格)
signature	firma	签名
sign-out	registro de salida	症状-外面
software	software	软件
speaker	altavoz	演说者
sprinkler system	sistema de rociadores	喷撒系统
stairs	escaleras	楼梯
stamp	estampilla	邮票
stapler	engrapadora	订书机
stationery	estacionamiento	信纸
steps	escalones	步
storage	depósito	存储
supplies	suministros	供应
system	sistema	系统
switch	interruptor	开关
table	mesa	桌子
tape	cinta	磁带
tape recorder	grabador de cinta	磁带录音机
telephone	teléfono	电话
television	televisión	电视
terminal	terminal	接线端
thumbtack	tachuela	图钉
vacuum cleaner	aspiradora	更干净的空间
VCR (video cassette recorder)	video cassettera	视频盒子录音机
vending machine	máquina expendedora	贩卖的机器
voice mail, voice message	mensaje de voz	声音邮件,声音消息
water cooler	bebedero	水冷却器
water fountain	fuente	水源泉

WORDS AT WORK	PALABRA DEL TRABAJO	在工作词汇
ability	habilidad	能力
absent	ausente	缺席
access	acceso	存取
accident	accidente	事故
accommodate	acomodar	接纳
accountability	contabilidad	负责
accounting	contable	会计学
action	acción	行动
adjustment	ajuste	调整
advancement	fomento	晋升
advertise	anuncia	做广告
advertisement	anuncio	广告
advice	consejo	建议
advise	aconsejar	劝告
advisor	consejero	顾问
affirmative action	acción afirmativa	赞成的行动
agency	agencia	机构
agent	agente	代理人
agreement	acuerdo	同意
allowed	permitido	允许
ambition	ambición	雄心
appearance	apariencia	出现
applicant	candidato	申请人
application	solicitud	申请
apply	solicitar	适用
appointment	cita	约会
appraisal	evaluación	估价
apprentice	aprendiz	徒弟
approval	aprobación	赞同
approve	aprobar	同意
aptitude	aptitud	才能
area	área	区域
arrangement	arreglo	整理
assistance	asistencia	帮助

assistant	asistente	助手
at all times	todas las veces	所有时间
attendance	asistencia	出席
attitude	actitud	态度
authority	autoridad	权威
authorization	autorización	授权
authorize	autorizar	批准
availability	disponibilidad	可用性
available	disponible	可得到
behavior	conducta	行为
benefit	beneficio	利益
billing	facturación	收费
boss	jefe	老板
building	edificio	大楼
business	negocio	商业
cafeteria	cafetería	自助食堂
career	carrera	职业
check, cheque	cheque	支票，支票
class, classes	clases	班，班
cleanliness	limpieza	干净
client	cliente	顾客
clientele	clientela	顾客
coach	entrenar	客车
colleague	colega	同事
college	colegio	学院
comment	comentario, observación	评价
commerce	comercio	商业
commercial	comercial	商业
committee	comité	委员会
communicate, communication	comunicar, comunicación	交流，通讯
company	compañía	同伴
compensate	compensar	补偿
compensation	compensación	补偿
compete	competir	竞争
competent	competente	有能力
competition	competición	竞争

competitor	competidor	竞争者
complaint	queja	抱怨
conduct	conducta	行为
conference	confcrencia	会议
conference room	salón de conferencias	会议房间
confidential	confidencial	秘密
conflict	conflicto	冲突
conflict of interest	conflicto de intereses	利益冲突
consensus	consenso	一致
consent	consentir	赞成
consideration	consideración	考虑
contact	contacto	接触
convenience	conveniencia	便利
convenient	conveniente	方便
corporate	de la empresa	社团
corporation	corporación	公司
cost	costo	费用
counsel, counseling	consejo, aconsejar	法律顾问, 建议
course	curso	路线
courteous	atento, cortés	谦恭
courtesy	cortesía	谦恭
coverage	cobertura	覆盖
co-worker	compañero dc trabajo	同事
criminal record	antecedente criminal	犯罪的记录
culture	cultura	文化
custodial	custodia	保管
customer service	servicio de atención al cliente	顾客服务
daily	diariamente	每日
damage	daño	损坏
date	fecha	日期
day-to-day	día a día	日常
deduction	deducción	推理
delivery	reparto	交货
dental	dental	牙科
department	departamento	部门
department head	mando del departamento	部门头

deposit	deposito	沉积物
description	descripción	描述
diploma	diploma	证书
disability	discapacidad	残疾
disciplinary action	acción disciplinaria	纪律的行动
discipline	disciplina	纪律
discrimination	discriminación	辨别
discuss	discutir	讨论
discussion	discusión	讨论
dismiss	despedir	解除
dismissal	despido	打发
distribute	distribuir	散布
distribution	distribución	分发
diversity	diversidad	差异
document, documented	documento, documentado	文件, 记录
downsize	reducción de personal	缩小
dress	indumentaria	衣服
dress code	código de indumentaria	衣服代码
driver's license	licencia de conducir	司机 许可证
drug test	prueba de detección de drogas	药测试
duty, duties	deber, deberes	税, 责任
education	educación	教育
effort	esfuerzo	努力
electronic	electrónico	电子
eligible, eligibility	elegible, elegibilidad	符合条件, 适任
employ	emplear	雇用
employee	empleado	雇员
employer	empleador	老板
environment	ambiente	环境
equal employment opportunity		
iguales oportunidades de empleo		相等的雇用机会
equity	equidad	公平
ethic	ética	伦理
ethical	ético	伦理
evaluate	evaluar	估计
evaluation	evaluación	评估

examination	examen	检查
exception	excepción	例外
excess, excessive	exceso, excesivo	过量, 过分
exempt	exento	除外
exemption	excepción	解脱
expectation	expectativa	期待
expense	gasto	费用
experience	experiencia	经验
factory	fábrica	工厂
failure	falla	失败
feedback	retroalimentación	反应
finance	fianza	金融
fire	fuego	火
firm	firma	公司
floor	piso	地板
foreign	extranjero	外国
franchise	franquicia	公民权
full-time	tiempo completo	专职
future	futuro	将来
goal	meta	球门
graduate	graduado	毕业生
green card	tarjeta verde	绿卡
grooming	acicalamiento	推荐
group	grupo	团体
growth	crecimiento	生长
handbook	manual	手册
harassment	acoso	骚扰
health	salud	健康
high school	secundaria	高中
hire	contratar	雇用
hiring	contrato	雇用
holiday	vacaciones	假期
human resources	recursos humanos	人力资源
hygiene	higiene	卫生
identification card	tarjeta de identificación	鉴定卡片
identity	identidad	身份

immediate	inmediato	立即
immediately	inmediatamente	很快地
immigrant	inmigrante	移民
immigration	inmigración	移民
impression	impresión	印象
improvement	mejora	改进
inappropriate	inapropiado	不适当
incident	incidente	事件
income	ingresos	收入
income tax	ingresos de renta	所得税
industrial	industrial	工业
industry	industrial	工业
inform	informe	通知
information	información	信息
initiative	iniciativa	行动
injury	herida	伤害

Immigration and Naturalization Service
Servicio de inmigración y Naturalización   移民和入国籍服务

inspect	inspector	视察
inspection	inspección	检查
instruct, instructor	instruir, instructor	指示, 讲师

insubordinate, insubordination
insubordinado, insubordinación   不听话, 反抗

insurance	seguro	保险
intention	intención	意图
intervene	intervenga	介入
intervention	intervención	干扰
interview	entrevista	会见
intimidate	intimide	胁迫
intimidation	intimidación	恐吓
inventory	inventario	库存
investigate	investigue	调查

investigation	investigación	调查
investment	inversión	投资
issue	problema	问题
job	trabajo	工作
job application	aplicación del trabajo	工作申请
job opening	apertura del trabajo	工作空缺
jury duty	deber del jurado	陪审团税
knowledge	conocimiento	知识
language	idioma	语言
leader	líder	领导人
leave of absence	licencia temporal	度假
legal	legal	合法
legal resident	residente legal	合法的居民
life insurance	seguro de vida	生活保险
lost and found	objetos perdidos	丧失并且发现
lunch, lunchroom	almuerzo, merendero	午餐, 速简餐厅
maintenance	mantenimiento	保持
management	dirección	管理
manager	gerente	经理
mandatory	obligatorio	命令
manufacturing	fabricando	生产
marital status	estado matrimonial	姻缘的状况
market	mercado	市场
marketing	comercializando	行销
material	material	原料
materiel	material	物资
medical	médico	医药
meeting	encontrándose	会议
merit	mérito	优点
method	método	方法
minimum wage	salario mínimo	最低工资
mission	misión	使命
monitor	monitor	监视
mother tongue	lengua madre	母语
multicultural	multicultural	文化丰富
national	nacional	国家

nationality	nacionalidad	国籍
neatness	prolijidad	整洁
no smoking	no fumar	禁止吸烟
non-smoking	área de no fumadores	非吸烟
notice	aviso	注意
notification	notificación	通知
notify	notifique	通报
objective	objetivo	目的
observation	observación	观察
occupation	ocupación	职业
off-duty	fuera de servicio	下班
offence	ofensa	冒犯
offensive	ofensiva	不开心
on-duty	en servicio	在责任上
opening	abriendo	开
operations	funcionamientos	军事行动
order	orden	顺序
organization	organización	组织
organize	organizar	组织
outline	bosquejo	轮廓
overtime	hora extras	过时
packaging	empaquetando	包装
parking	estacionando	停车
participate	participar	加入
participation	participación	参予
part-time	tiempo parcial	业余时间
pay day	día de pago	付白天
payroll	nómina	工资单
percentage	porcentaje	百分比
perform, performance	desempeñar, desempeño	演出,表现
permanent	permanente	永久
permission	permiso	权限
permit	permitir	许可证
personal	personal	私人
personnel	personal	职员
physical	físico	物理

plant	planta	植物
policy	política	政策
position	posición	位置
potential	potencial	潜在
practice	practicar	实践
prejudice	prejuicio	偏见
premises	premisas	房屋
present	presente	现在
privacy	retiro	隐私
private	privado	私人
probation	probación	检验
problem	problema	问题
procedure	procedimiento	步骤
process	proceso	过程
product	producto	产品
production	producción	生产
profession	profesión	职业
professional	profesional	职业
program	programa	节目
promote	promueva	促进
promotion	promoción	促进
property	propiedad	属性
protection	protección	保护
protective clothing	ropa de protección	防护的衣服
provide	proporcionar	提供
provision	provisión	预备
public	público	公共
public relations (PR)	relaciones públicas (PR)	公共的关系
punch	perforar	穿孔机
punch card	tarjeta perforada	穿孔卡片
punctual, punctuality	puntual, puntualidad	守时, 准时
qualification	calificación	合格
qualify	calificar	限制
quality	calidad	质量
question	pregunta	问题
questionnaire	encuesta	问询表

quit	renunciar	停止
quitting time	tiempo de renuncia	停止时间
raise	aumento	涨
receiving	recibiendo	收到
reception	recepción	接收
recommendation	recomendación	建议
recruit	reclutar	成员
reference	referencia	参考
referral	referencia	工作分派
regulation	regulación	规则
replacement	reemplazo	代替
report	informe	报告
represent	represente	代表
representative	representante	代表
request	demanda	请求
require	requerir	no translation
requirement	requisito	要求
resign	resignar	辞职
resignation	resignación	辞职
responsibility	responsabilidad	责任
restrict	restringir	限制
restricted	restringido	限制
result, results	resultado, resultados	结果, 结果
resumé	curriculum vitae	履历
retire, retirement	retiro, jubilación	退休, 退休
review	revisión	回顾
rights	derechos	权利
role	papel, rol	角色
room	cuarto, habitación	空间
rule	regla	统治
salary	sueldo	薪金
sale	venta	出售
sales tax	impuestos a las ventas	出售税
satisfaction	satisfacción	满足
schedule	horario	时间表
screening process	proceso de reclutamiento	屏蔽过程

seasonal	estacional	周期性
secretarial	de secretaria	书记
secretary	secretaria	秘书
security	seguridad	安全
service	servicio	服务
sexual harassment	acoso sexual	性别的骚扰
shift	turno	移动
shipping	despacho	发货
shop	comprar	商店
sign	firmar	症状
signature	firma	签名
skill	habilidad	技能
smoke, smoking	fumar, fumando	烟，吸烟
Social Security	Seguridad social	社会的安全
solution	solución	解决办法
sponsor	patrocinador	赞助
staff	personal	职员
staffroom	sala de profesores	no translation
standard	normal	标准
station	estación	车站
step-by-step	paso a paso	逐步
stereotype	stereotipo	老套
store	tienda	店
study, studying	estudiar, estudiando	学习，学习
subordinate	subordinado	从属
success	éxito	成功
successful	exitoso	成功
suggestion	sugerencia	建议
suggestion box	caja de la sugerencia	建议盒子
superintendent	superintendente	主管
support	apoyo	支持
tardy, tardiness	tardío, la tardanza	缓慢，迟缓
team, teamwork	equipo, trabajo en equipo	队，协作
technical	técnico	技术
technique	técnica	技术
temporary	temporal	暂时

terminate	despedir	停止
termination	despido	结束
test, testing	prueba, probando	测试, 测试
theft	robo	偷窃
time	tiempo	时间
time card	tarjeta de tiempo	时间卡片
time clock	reloj de tiempo	时间钟
train	tren	火车
trainee	aprendiz	实习生
training	entrenando	训练
transfer	traslado	转移
transportation	transporte	交通
tuition	matricula	学费
type, typing	tipear, tipeando	类型, 打
uniform	uniforme	制服
university	universidad	大学
vacancy	vacante	空缺
vacant	libre	空白
vacation	vacación	假期
violation	violación	违反
visible	visible	可见
waiting list	lista de espera	等待的列表
warehouse	el almacén	仓库
weekend	fin de semana	周末
withdraw	retirar	撤退
work experience	experiencia de trabajo	工作经验
work hours	horas de trabajo	工作小时
work visa	visa de trabajo	工作签证
work, to work	trabajo, trabajar	工作, 工作
workday	día laborable	工作日
workplace	lugar de trabajo	工作场所
zone	zona	地区

BUSINESS TERMS (RETAIL)	CONDICIONES COMERCIALES (AL POR MENOR)	交换条件 (零售)
advertisement	anuncio	广告
back order	devolución	过期订单
billboard	cartelera	告示板
brand	marca	商标
brochure	folleto	手册
budget	presupuesto	预算
buy	compra	买
cash flow	movimiento de tesorería	现金流动
catalogue	catálogo	目录
claim	demanda	宣称
clearance	despacho de aduanas	清除
commercial	comercial	商业
competition	competición	竞争
consignment	envío	交托
customer	cliente	顾客
damaged	dañado	损坏
design	plan	设计
designer	diseñador	设计者
discount	descuento	折扣
down payment	pago al contado	首期款
duty free	libre de impuestos	免费的税
estimate	estimación	估计
excluded	excluido	排除
export	exportación	出口
flyer	aviador	飞行员
free	gratuito	免费
half-price	mitad de precio	半价
imported	importado	进口
included	incluido	包括
installment	instalación	款项
invoice	factura	发票
label	etiqueta	标签
lay away	dejar algo reservado	离开躺
logo	logotipo	标识语

loss	pérdida	损失
mail order	orden del correo	邮购
manufacturer	fabricante	制造商
mark-down	rebaja	削价
mark-up	encarecimiento	标注
merchandise	mercancía	货物
on account	a cuenta	在帐目上
order	orden	顺序
overdue	retrasado	过期
packaging	empaquetando	包装
paid	pagado	付钱
paid in full	totalmente pagado	付钱了在完整
patent	patente	获专利
pay	pagar	no translation
payment plan	plan de pago	报酬计划
price	precio	价格
profit	ganancia	利益
promotion	promoción	促进
quantity	cantidad	数量
rebate	rebaja	减少
receipt	recibo	收据
reduced	reducido	减少
reduction	reducción	降低
refund	reintegro	退款
retail	al por menor	零卖
sale	venta	no translation
sales pitch	rollo publicitario	出售沥青
sales tax	impuesto sobre las ventas	出售税
salesperson	vendedor	销售人员
sample	muestra	样品
seasonal	estacional	周期性
self-service	autoservicio	自助式
sell	venda	卖
shipment	embarque	载运
spend	gastar	花费
stamp	sello	邮票

subtotal	subtotal	小计
supply	suministro	供应
tax free	libre de impuestos	免费的税
total	total	全部
trade	comercio	no translation
trademark	marca registrada	商标
used	usado	使用
void	nulo	空旷
wholesale	venta al por mayor	趸售

INTERVIEW QUESTIONS   LAS PREGUNTAS DE LA ENTREVISTA 会见问题

Do you speak English?

   ¿Usted habla inglés?   你说话英语吗？

Are you a legal resident in the United States?

   ¿Usted es un residente legal en los Estados Unidos?
   你是美国合法的居民吗？

Do you have legal documents to work in the United States?

   ¿Usted tiene los documentos legales para trabajar en los Estados Unidos?
   你有在美国工作的合法的文件吗？

Do you have a green card?

   ¿Usted tiene una tarjeta verde?   你有一张绿卡吗？

Do you have any experience with this type of work?

   ¿Usted tiene cualquier experiencia con este tipo de trabajo?
   你有任何这类工作的经验吗？

What skills do you have for this job?

   ¿Qué habilidades usted tiene por este trabajo?
   你有什么关于这份工作的技能？

Do you have references?

¿Usted tiene referencias?　　　　　　　你有介绍和参考吗？

Do you have a resumé?

¿Usted tiene un curriculum vitae?　　你有简历吗？

Please fill out this application form.

Por favor llene este formulario de aplicación.
请填写申请表格.

Are you willing to work evenings/weekends/night shift?

¿Usted esta dispuesto a trabajar en turnos de noche y fines de semana?
你愿意晚上/周末/晚上加班？

Do you have a driver's license?

¿Tiene licencia para manejar?　　　　你有一个驾照吗？

Where do you live?

¿Dónde vive?　　　　　　　　　　　你在哪儿生活？

Do you have your own transportation?

¿Tiene su propio transporte?　　　　　你有自己的交通工具吗？

This is a part-time/full-time job.

Éste es un trabajo de tiempo parcial/tiempo completo.
.这是一份兼职/全职工作.

This job is for seasonal work.

Este trabajo es por temporada.　　　　这份工作为周期性的工作.

The pay is ＿＿ dollars an hour.

La paga es de ＿＿ dólares por hora.　薪水是 美元一个小时.

I'm sorry, we don't have any openings.

Yo lo siento, nosotros no tenemos ninguna apertura.
抱歉的, 我们穿上 有任何洞.

The position has been filled.

El cargo ya ha sido ocupado. 职位已经满了.

I/We will let you know.

Le haré/haremos saber. 我/我们将让你熟悉.

Where/how can we contact you?

¿Dónde y cómo nosotros podemos avisarle?
在哪儿/怎么我们能联系你?

Please leave your phone number.

Por favor deje su número de teléfono. 请留下你的电话号码.

Do you have a high school diploma?

¿Tiene diploma de la escuela secundaria?
你有高中毕业证吗?

Do you have a college degree?

¿Tiene título universitario? 你有大学学历吗?

Do you have special training for this job?

¿Usted tiene el entrenamiento especial para este trabajo?
你接受过专门的职业训练吗?

Why do you want this job?

¿Por qué usted quiere este trabajo? 你为什么想要这份工作?

Why should we hire you for this job?

¿Por qué nosotros debemos contratarlo para este trabajo?
我们为什么雇用你做这份工作?

Can you come in for an (another) interview?

¿Puede venir a otra entrevista? 你进行一 (另外一个) 会见?

Why did you leave your last job?

¿Por qué usted dejó su último trabajo? 你为什么辞掉最后一份工作?

How long did you work at your last job?

¿Cuánto tiempo usted trabajó en su último trabajo?

你从事最后一份工作多长时间？

Are you currently employed/working?

¿Usted esta actualmente con trabajo/empleado?

你是否在职呢？

There is a three-month (90-day) probationary period.

El periodo de prueba es de 90 días.　　　　有3月 (90天) 试用期.

Can you work holidays and weekends?

¿Usted puede trabajar fiestas y fines de semana?

你能在假期和周末工作吗？

Are you willing to work overtime if necessary?

¿Está dispuesto a trabajar horas extras si es necesario?

如果必要你愿意加班吗？

When can you start/begin?

¿Cuándo puede comenzar?　　　　什么时候能你开始/开始？

Do you have any questions?

¿Usted tiene alguna pregunta?　　　　你有任何问题吗？

Please be here by ___ o'clock.

Por favor esté aquí a las ___horas.　　　　请到这里在 时间.

We would like you to start right away/next week/on Monday.

Nos gustaría que usted empezara ya/la próxima semana/el lunes.

我们想你开始工作 立刻/下一周/星期一.

Why do you want to work here?

¿Por qué usted quiere trabajar aquí?　　　　你为什么想要在这里工作？

Thank you for your time.

Gracias por su tiempo. 打搅您了.

You must wear a uniform.

Usted debe llevar un uniforme. 你必须穿一身制服.

We will provide you with a uniform.

Nosotros le proporcionaremos un uniforme.
我们将向你提供一身制服.

You must buy your own uniform.

Usted debe comprar su propio uniforme.
你必须买自己的制服.

Your uniform must be clean before each shift.

Su uniforme debe estar limpio antes de cada turno.
在每次轮班前你的制服一定要保持干净.

You must wear a name tag.

Usted debe llevar una etiqueta con el nombre.
你必须佩戴一个身份名片.

You will be trained before you start working.

Usted se entrenará antes de que usted empiece a trabajar.
在你开始工作以前你将接受培训.

Personal grooming/appearance/hygiene is important for this job.

La apariencia/higiene personal es importante para este trabajo.
个人装扮/外表/卫生干净 对于这个工作重要.

The possession or use of drugs or alcohol on the job is cause for dismissal.

La posesión o uso de drogas o alcohol en el trabajo es causa de despido.
在工作期间吸毒或喝酒将给予解雇.

Will you consent to a drug test?

¿Estaría dispuesto hacerse una prueba de drogas?

你愿意进行一次测试吗?

We conduct regular random drug testing.

Nosotros exigimos regularmente pruebas de drogas.

我们进行物规则的测试.

You are allowed a 15-minute break during your shift.

Tiene permitido 15 minutos de descanso durante su turno.

你能有15分钟休息在你的轮班期间.

You must call if you will be late or absent.

Usted debe llamar si usted llegará tarde o ausente.

如果你将迟到, 那么你必须打电话通知.

The company does/does not provide medical/dental insurance.

La compañía no/si proporciona seguro de médico/dental.

公司提供/不提供医疗保险.

There is no-smoking in the building/on the job.

No se puede fumar en el edificio de trabajo.

在在大楼/上有没有吸工作.

You will have a half-hour/hour lunch break.

Usted tendrá media hora/una hora de almuerzo.

在在大楼/上有没有吸工作.

Your supervisor will tell you your job duties.

Su supervisor le dirá sus deberes de trabajo.

你的监督人将告诉你你的工作责任.

Your supervisor is _____.

Su supervisor es _____.   你的监督人是.

Payday is every week/two weeks on (Friday).

El día de pago es todas las semanas/cada dos semanas los (viernes).

发薪日是每个星期/2星期在上(星期五).

I would like to check these references.

Me gustaría verificar estas referencias.   我想检查这些参考书.

How did you hear about this job?

¿Cómo usted oyó hablar de este trabajo?   ?你怎么听说了这份工作?

Try again next month.

Intente el próximo mes de nuevo.   再试用下个月.

I'm sorry, we're not hiring.

Yo lo siento, nosotros no estamos contratando.

我是抱歉的, 我们是不雇用.

Please take a seat.

Por favor tome asiento.   请占一个位子.

Sorry to keep you waiting.

Discúlpeme por hacerlo esperar.   抱歉让你等待.

ON-THE-JOB CONDUCT   LA CONDUCTA EN EL TRABAJO   工作规范

You are prohibited from working under the influence of drugs or alcohol.

Prohibido trabajar bajo la influencia de drogas o alcohol.

你禁止受药或者酒精的影响工作.

There is no smoking in the building or while in uniform.

No se permite fumar en el edificio o mientras se esta trabajando.

不可以在大楼或穿制服时吸烟.

There is to be no fraternization with the guests.

No relacionarse íntimamente con los clientes.

不得与客人有亲密关系.

Damaging or stealing guest or company property will result in dismissal.

Dañar o robar a clientes o propiedades de la compañía serán causa despido.

损坏或者偷窃客人或者公司财产将给予解雇.

There is no sleeping while on duty.

No se puede dormir en servicio.

上班时不可以睡觉.

You may not leave work during working hours without permission from a supervisor.

Usted no puede dejar el trabajo durante las horas de trabajo sin el permiso de un supervisor.

没有上级的许可, 在工作时间你不可以擅自离岗.

Firearms and weapons are prohibited on the premises.

Se prohíben armas de fuego.

禁止拥有武器.

Solicitation of guests or employees is prohibited during working hours.

La solicitación de clientes o empleados se prohíbe durante las horas de trabajo.

禁止在工作时间处理客人或者雇员的恳求.

Sexual harassment of guests or employees will result in termination.

El acoso sexual de clientes o empleados producirá el despido.

禁止对客人或者员工进行性骚扰.

You must report for your shift on time.

Usted debe informar a tiempo para un cambio de turno.

你必须准时报告你的变化情况.

You must notify your supervisor if you will be late or absent.

Usted debe notificar a su supervisor si usted llegará tarde o ausente.

你如果迟到或缺席，你应该向上级报告.

All meals must be eaten in the employee cafeteria.

Todas las comidas deben comerse en la cafetería de empleados.

员工只允许在员工食堂进餐.

You must use the employee entrance to enter and exit the building.

Usted debe usar la entrada del empleado para entrar y salir del edificio.

你只能从员工入口进出办公大楼.

You must wear your name tag while on duty.

Usted debe llevar su etiqueta del nombre mientras este en servicio.

当班时，你必须佩戴你的身份证件.

You must report any found items immediately.

Usted debe informar si encontró artículos inmediatamente.

你必须立即报告一切发现的情况.

Visiting with friends and relatives while on duty is not allowed.

La visita de amigos y parientes no se permite mientras se este en servicio.

当上班不允许拜访朋友和亲戚.

You must give two-weeks notice when resigning.

Usted debe avisar con dos semanas de anticipación si quiere renunciar.

提出辞职，你必须提前两周通知公司.

You must attend all scheduled staff meetings.

Usted debe asistir a todas las reuniones del personal.

你必须参加所有员工需要参加的会议.

You must provide your own lock for your employee locker.

Usted debe mantener su propia cerradura en su cajón del empleado.

你需要自己提供锁为你的贮物柜.

You must notify your supervisor within 48 hours of being injured at work.

Usted debe notificar a su supervisor dentro de 48 horas de dañarse al trabajo.

在工作中受伤, 你必须在48小时内通知你的上级.

You must have a clean and neat appearance.

Usted debe tener una apariencia limpia y aseada.

你必须着装干净整洁.

GENERAL INSTRUCTIONS   LAS INSTRUCCIONES GENERALES   一般介绍

This is the procedure.

Éste es el procedimiento.   这是 手续.

This is what I want done.

Esto es lo que yo quiero hecho.   这是我想做的.

Please do it this way.

Por favor hágalo esta manera.   请按这个办法做.

Don't touch it.

No lo toque.   别接触它.

Be very careful.

Tenga mucho cuidado.   很小心.

It's a mistake.

Es un error.   这是一个错误.

Please try it again.

Por favor pruébelo de nuevo.   请再试一次.

We are open at _____.

Nosotros estamos abiertos a _____.   我们是公开的在_____.

We are closed on -.
    Nosotros estamos cerrados a -.   我们是关闭在-.

Please be here by -.
    Por favor esté aquí por -.   请通过 到这里来-.

You start at -.
    Usted empieza a -.   你出发在 -.

You finish at -.
    Usted termina a -.   你完成在-.

Take a break at -.
    Tome un descanso a -.   在 休息一下-.

Follow the instructions.
    Siga las instrucciones.   接着介绍.

Read the manual.
    Lea el manual.   阅读手册.

Look at the picture.
    Mire el cuadro.   看图片.

This is our system.
    Éste es nuestro sistema.   这是我们的系统.

Ask for help.
    Pida ayuda.   请求帮助.

Check the inventory.
    Verifique el inventario.   检查详细目录.

Lock the door when you leave.
    Cierre con llave la puerta cuando usted sale.
当你离开时请锁门.

Set the alarm with the code.
    Ponga la alarma con el código.   用代号设置铃.

There is a problem.
    Hay un problema.   有一个问题.

Ask me if you don't understand.
    Pregúnteme si usted no entiende.   如果你不理解请问我.

There is more work to do.
    Hay más trabajo para hacer.   有更多工作要做.

Turn off the machine.
    Apague la máquina.   关掉机器.

Put everything away.
    Guarde todo.   放下所有的事.

Clean up the mess.
    Limpie el desorden.   把脏乱整理号.

Check the temperature.
    Verifique la temperatura.   检查温度.

TESTING/EVALUATING	**EVALUANDO**	测试/评估
ability	habilidad	能力
abuse	abuso	滥用
achievement	logro	成就
advancement	avance	进步
alternative	alternativa	另外
analyze, analysis	analizar, análisis	分析
appearance	apariencia	出现
appraise, appraisal	apreciar, apreciación	评估
appreciation	apreciación	欣赏

appropriate	apropiado	适当
approval	aprobación	赞同
approve	apruebe	同意
argumentative	argumentativo	争论的
attitude	actitud	态度
average	promedio	平均
bad mood	mal humor	坏的坏脾气
behavior	conducta	行为
better	mejor	更好
clarification	clarificación	净化
commendation	alabanza	赞扬
commitment	compromiso	许诺
committee	comité	委员会
communication	comunicación	交流,沟通
competition	competición	竞争
complaint	queja	抱怨
complement	complemento	补助
complete	completo	完全
compliment	cumplimiento	称赞
conduct	conducta	行为
confident, confidence	seguro, confianza	自信
confidential	confidencial	秘密
confidentiality	confidcncialidad	机密性
conflict	conflicto	冲突
constructive	constructivo	建设性
cooperation	cooperación	协作
creative	creativo	有创造性
decision-making	tomando una decisión	决策
demoted	degradado	使降职
demotion	degradación	降级
desire	deseo	欲望
develop	desarrollar	开发
development	desarrollo	发展
effective	eficaz	有效
efficient	eficaz	有效
effort	esfuerzo	努力

encourage	animar	鼓励
enthusiasm	entusiasmo	热情
enthusiastic	entusiasmado	热情
error	error	误差
evaluation	evaluación	评估
examiner	examinador	主考人
example	ejemplo	例子
exceed	exceder	超过
excellent	excelente	优秀
exhibit	exhibición	展出
expectation	expectativa	期待
expertise	especialización	专家知识
fair	justo	公平
final decision	decisión definitiva	最终决定
fired	despedido	雇佣
follow-up	seguimiento	后接
foul language	vocabulario inapropiado	污秽的语言
goal	meta	球门
good mood	buen humor	好的坏脾气
grade	calidad	等级
growth	crecimiento	生长
harassment	acoso	骚扰
high	alto	高
identify	identificar	鉴别
implement	instrumentar	实现
improper	impropio	不适合
improve	mejorar	改善
improvement	mejora	改进
incentive	incentivo	动机
incomplete	incompleto	不完善
independent	independiente	独立
inefficient	ineficaz	效率差
initiative	iniciativa	行动
inspection	inspección	检查
instructions	instrucciones	说明
intelligence	inteligencia	智力

interrupt	interrupción	打断
investigation	investigación	调查
issue	problema	问题
job performance	actuación del trabajo	工作成绩
job skill	habilidad del trabajo	工作技能
knowledge	conocimiento	知识
language	idioma	语言
late	tarde	晚
lead	primacía	领导
leader	líder	领导人
less than expected	menos de lo esperado	不到期待
limitation	limitación	局限性
loitering	perdiendo el tiempo	徘徊
lower than hoped	mas bajo de lo esperado	没有预期好
maintain	mantener	维持
maximum	máximo	最大
measure	medida	测量
minimum	mínimo	最小
missing	extrañando	失去
mistake	error	错误
model	modelo	模型
morale	moral	民心
more	más	更
motivated	motivado	激发
motivation	motivación	动机
needs improvement	la mejora de necesidades	需要改进
need	necesitar	需要
negative	negativo	否定
objective	objetivo	目的
observe	observar	观察
organized	organizado	组织
outstanding	excelente	显著
patience	paciente	耐性
personnel file	archivo del personal	职员文件
poor	pobre	差
positive	positivo	积极的

potential	potencial	潜在
prepare	preparar	准备
prepared	preparado	准备
pre-test	prueba previa	预告测验
pride	orgullo	骄傲
priority	prioridad	优先
probation	aprobación	检验
problem	problema	问题
process	proceso	过程
production	producción	生产
productive	productivo	生产
professional	profesional	职业
professionalism	profesionalismo	职业特性
progress	progreso	进步
punctual	puntual	守时
quality	calidad	质量
quality control	control de la calidad	质量控制
reaction time	máquina para empaquetar	反应时间
record	registro	记录
reinforce	refuerzo	加固
repeat	repetir	重复
report	informe	报告
reprimand	reprimenda	责备
resign	renunciar	辞职
resignation	renuncia	辞职
responsibility	responsabilidad	责任
results	resultados	结果
review	revisión	回顾
reward	premio	报酬
satisfactory	satisfactorio	圆满
satisfied	satisfecho	满足
score	puntaje	分数
search	búsqueda	搜索
self-improvement	mejorar por sí mismo	自我改造
self-motivated	motivarse a sí mismo	激发自我
service	servicio	服务

situation	situación	状况
solution	solución	解决办法
spirit	espíritu	精神
standards	normas	标准
strategy	estrategia	策略
strength	fuerza	力量
study	estudio	学习
substandard	inferior	非标准语言
success	éxito	成功
suggestion	sugerencia	建议
support	apoyo	支持
surveillance	vigilancia	监控
suspended	suspendido	推迟
suspension	suspensión	挂
talent	talento	才能
tardy	tardío	缓慢
technique	técnica	技术
test	prueba	no translation
theft	robo	偷窃
time management	tiempo gerencial	时间管理
track record	registro de la huella, trayectoria	记载
trainer	entrenador	训练员
transferred	transferido	转移
trouble	problema	麻烦
troublemaker	problemático	惹麻烦的人
unacceptable	inaceptable	无法接受
vandalism	vandalismo	破坏
violent	violento	强烈
weakness	debilidad	软弱
witness	testigo	证人
worse	más peor	更坏

Do your best.	Haga lo mejor.	尽最大努力.
Don't be nervous.	No esté nervioso.	别紧张.

Can you explain this?   ¿Usted puede explicar esto?   你能解释这吗？

Are you aware there is a problem?
¿Usted es consciente que hay un problema?
你知道有一个问题？

What can we do to fix it?
¿Qué podemos hacer para arreglarlo?   我们能做什么修理它？

How can you improve?
¿Cómo usted puede mejorar?   你能怎么改善？

What do you suggest?
¿Qué sugiere?   你什么建议？

I'd like to hear your ideas.
Me gustaría oír sus ideas.   我想听见你的想法.

How do you feel about it?
¿Cómo se siente usted sobre esto?   关于它你感觉到怎么样？

What are your goals?
¿Cuáles son sus metas?   你的球门是什么？

What is your opinion?
¿Cuál es su opinión?   你的意见是什么？

In my opinion...
En mi opinión...   按照我的看法看法...

Let's resolve this issue.
Resolvamos este problema.   让我们这期解决.

You're part of the team.
Usted es parte del equipo.   你是团队的一部分.

What a great job!
¡Eso que un gran trabajo!　　　　　　　多么好的工作！

Good work!	¡Buen trabajo!	好工作！
Very good.	Muy bueno.	很好.
You can do it!	¡Usted puede hacerlo!	你能做它！
Thanks for your help.	Gracias por su ayuda.	谢谢你的帮助.
I like your attitude.	Me gusta su actitud.	我喜欢你的态度.
Great idea.	Gran idea.	伟大的想法.
I trust you.	Yo confío en usted.	我信任你.

You are a fast learner.
Usted es un aprendiz rápido.　　　　　你是一名快的学习者.

You show great potential.
Usted muestra un gran potencial.　　　你显示出伟大的潜力.

You need to work on this area.
Usted necesita trabajar en este área.　　你需要在这个区域上工作.

You are a valuable employee.
Usted es un valioso empleado.　　　　　你是一个有价值的雇员.

You are very efficient.
Usted es muy eficaz.　　　　　　　　　你是很有效的.

You can work independently.
Usted puede trabajar independientemente.　你能独立地工作.

You need more supervision.
Usted necesita más supervisión.　　　　你需要更多的监督.

You're ready to advance.
Usted está listo para avanzar/ascender.　你是准备好了更好的发展.

POST OFFICE	CORREO	邮局
address	dirección	地址
airmail	correo por avión	航空邮件
contents	contenidos	内容
customs	clientes	客户
customs form	formulario de clientes	客户表单
delivery	entrega	交货
document	documento	文件
envelope	sobre	信封
exchange	intercambio	交换
express	expreso	表达
fragile, breakable	frágil, rompible	脆的
ground, surface	terreno, superficie	地面, 水面
identification	identificación	鉴定
insurance, insured	seguro, asegurado	保险
letter	carta	信
mail	correo	邮件
metered mail	correo medido	测量邮件
overnight	toda la noche	一夜间
package	paquete	包裹
parcel	paquete	包裹
parcel notice	el aviso del paquete	包裹通知
post office box	apartado postal	邮政信箱
postage paid	estampilla paga	邮资支付
postcard	tarjeta postal	明信片
printed matter	impresos	印刷品
receipt	recibo	收据
registered	registrado	登记
return address	dirección del retorno	返回地址
shipping	enviando	发货
shipping label	etiqueta de envío	发货单
signature	firma	签名
stamp	estampilla	邮票

What is inside?
   ¿Qué hay adentro?   什么在里面？

How many days will it take?

¿Cuántos días tardará?　　　　　　　　多少天能拿到它？

Do you need a receipt?

¿Usted necesita un recibo?　　　　　　你需要一张收条吗？

How much does it weigh?

¿Cuánto pesa?　　　　　　　　　　　　它重多少？

Please fill out this label/form.

Por favor llene este formulario.　　　请充满o音阶第一音这标签/形式.

How do you wish to send this?

¿Cómo usted desea enviar esto?　　　你想怎样发送它？

I would like to send it registered mail.

Me gustaría enviarle correo certificado.　我想送登记邮件.

I would like to send it by airmail.

Me gustaría enviarlo por avión.　　　　我想用航空邮件寄它.

I would like to send it regular post.

Me gustaría enviarlo por correo regular.　我想按邮政规则寄送它.

What is the cheapest way to send it?

¿Cuál es la manera más barata de enviarlo?

什么是发送它的最便宜的方法？

I would like to insure the contents.

Me gustaría asegurar los contenidos.　我想确认这个内容.

It is breakable/fragile.　　Es frágil/rompible.　　它是会破的/脆的.

I'd like to buy some stamps, please.

Me gustaría comprar algunas estampillas por favor.

我想买一些邮票.

I'd like to send this parcel.

Me gustaría enviar este paquete.　　　　我想寄出这个包裹.

I'd like to pick up a parcel.

Me gustaría recoger un paquete.　　　　我想拿起一个包裹.

May I see some identification?

¿Tiene alguna identificación?　　　　我能看一些鉴定？

I'd like to open a post office box.

Me gustaría abrir un apartado postal.　　我想打开邮政信箱.

I have changed my address.

Yo he cambiado mi dirección.　　　　我已经更改了我的地址.

I would like to have my mail forwarded.

Me gustaría tener mi correo remitido.　　我想让人寄我的邮件.

TRANSPORTATION	TRANSPORTE	运输
airplane	avión	飞机
airport	aeropuerto	机场
automobile	automóvil	汽车
avenue	avenida	大街
bicycle path	senda de bicicleta	自行车道
board, boarding	embarcar, embarcando	木板
boat	barco	船
boulevard	bulevar	大道
bridge	puente	桥牌
bulldozer	excavadora	推土机
bus	autobús	公共汽车
bus stop	parada	汽车站
car	automóvil	汽车
cash	dinero en efectivo	现金
city block	cuadra	城区

coin	moneda	硬币
commercial vehicle	vehículo comercial	商业交通工具
delivery truck	camión de entrega	交货
disembark, disembarking	desembarcar, desembarcando	登陆, 登陆
downtown	centro de la ciudad	闹市区
economy	economía	经济
entrance	entrada	入口
exact change	cambio exacto	精确的变化
exit	salida	出口
express	expreso	表达
expressway	autopista	高速公路
fare	tarifa	费用
ferry	barca	运
first class	primera clase	头等
freeway	autopista	马路
highway	carretera	高速公路
interstate	interestatal	州际
itinerary	itinerario	指南
map	mapa	地图
non-smoking, smoking	prohibido fumar, se permite fumar	吸烟
off-ramp	vía de salida	离开斜坡
one-way	sentido/dirección/mano única	单程
on-ramp	vía de entrada	在斜坡上
outskirts	las afueras	郊区
overpass	paso a desnivel	天桥
parking lot	parque de estacionamiento	停车场
passenger	pasajero	旅客
pedway	pedway	步行桥
pick up truck	camioneta pick up	上卡车
platform	plataforma	月台
reserved	reservado	保留
return	retorno	回来
ride-on mower	paseo en segador	乘坐割草机
schedule	horario	时间表
seat	asiento	位子
sidewalk	acera	人行道

sign	señal	标志
streetcar	tranvía	电车
subway	metro	地铁
taxi, cab	taxi	出租车, 出租汽车
terminal	terminal	接线端
ticket	boleto	票
toll booth	cabina de peaje	使用费位子
tow truck	grúa remolque	拖车
tractor	tractor	拖拉机
traffic	tráfico	交通
traffic signal	semáforo	交通信号
train	tren	火车
train station	estación del tren	火车车站
tunnel	túnel	隧道
underpass	pasaje subterráneo	地道
van	carro de mudanzas	货车
vehicle	vehículo	交通工具
wicket, ticket window	boletería	小门, 票窗户
What number?	¿Qué número?	什么数字?
How much is it to ____?	¿Cuánto es _____?	它有多少 _____?
I want to go to ____.	Yo quiero ir a _____.	我想要走 _____.
How do I get to ____?	¿Cómo llego a _____?	我怎样到达 ____?

When (what time) does it leave?
    ¿Cuándo (qué hora) sale?   当时(什么时间) 离开?

How long will it take?
    ¿Cuánto tiempo tomará?   它有多长?

From what platform (does it leave)?
    ¿De qué plataforma (sale)?   从什么站台(离开)?

Where do I catch _____?
    ¿Dónde yo lo tomo _____?   在哪儿我上的 _____?

I need a map of the city.

　　Yo necesito un mapa de la ciudad.　　　　我需要城市的一张地图.

Can you give me directions to _____?

　　¿Usted puede guiarme a _____?　　　　能你给我指导吗 _____?

ON THE TELEPHONE　　　　EN EL TELÉFONO　　　　在电话

Hello?	¿Hola?	你好?
May I speak to...?	¿Puedo hablar con...?	我能对...说?
I'm sorry, s/he's not in.	Yo lo siento, el/ella no está.	抱歉的,她/他不在.
May I take a message?	¿Le quiere dejar un mensaje?	我能留个口信吗?
May I leave a message?	¿Puedo dejarle un mensaje?	我能留个口信吗?
Please call back.	Por favor vuelva a llamar.	请打电话回来.
Thank you very much.	Muchas gracias.	非常感谢你
Good-bye.	Adiós.	再见.
This is _____ speaking.	Quien le habla es _____.	这是 _____说.

I will call back later.

　　Yo volveré a llamar después.　　　　稍后我会打电话来的.

I will have him/her return your call.

　　Le devolveré su llamada.　　　　我会让他/她回你电话的.

I will give him/her the message.

　　Le daré el mensaje.　　　　我会给他/她留消息.

May I take your name and phone number?

　　¿Puedo tomar su nombre y número de teléfono?
　　我能记下你的名字和电话号码?

S/he is in a meeting/out of the office.

　　El/Ella está en una reunión/fuera de la oficina.
　　她/他在开会/离开办公室了.

S/he is on another line.

Él/ella está en otra línea.   她／他在在线.

Can you repeat that please?

¿Usted puede repetir por favor?   你能重复一遍吗？

Can you speak more slowly?

¿Puede hablar más despacio?   你说慢一点吗？

May I speak to your supervisor?

¿Puedo hablar a su supervisor?   我能和你的监督人说话吗？

I'm calling about...	Yo estoy llamando porque...	我正在打电话...
Tell him/her that...	Dígale que...	告诉他/她那...
One moment, please.	Un momento, por favor.	请等一会.
It's urgent.	Es urgente.	这是紧急事件.

I will have to put you on hold.

Yo tendré que ponerlo en la espera.   我必须和你保持联系.

Can you call back later?

¿Usted puede volver a llamar después?   你过一会能打电话来吗？

She/He doesn't work here.

Él/Ella no trabaja aquí.   她/他不在这里工作.

You have the wrong number.

Usted tiene el número equivocado.   你打错号了.

I'm sorry, I have the wrong number.

Yo lo siento, tengo un número equivocado.
我是抱歉的, 我打错号了.

Is this the correct number?

¿Es este el número correcto?   这是正确的号码吗？

What number are you dialing?

¿Qué número usted está marcando? 你拨的什么号？

The number has been changed.

El número se ha cambiado. 号码已经更改.

The line was disconnected.

La línea estaba desconectada. 掉线了.

The line is busy.	La línea está ocupada.	线路正忙.
Please hang up.	Por favor cuelgue.	请挂电话起来.
Wait for the tone.	Espere por el tono.	等待接通.

Leave a message at the tone.

Deje un mensaje al tono. 留下消息.

Try your call again.

Pruebe su llamada de nuevo. 在拨一次.

I'd like to make a collect call.

Me gustaría hacer una llamada con cobro revertido.
我想打通电话.

Do you accept the charges?

¿Usted acepta los cargos? 你接受这个费用吗？

AT A BANK	EN UN BANCO	在银行
account	cuenta	帐目
account number	número de cuenta	帐号
address	dirección	地址
approval	aprobación	赞同
asset	recurso	资产

ATM (automated teller machine)
ATM (la máquina del cajero automatizada)   自动取款机

balance	balance	帐目
bankruptcy	quiebra	破产
bill	factura	帐单
bond	bono	契约
branch	sucursal	分支
budget	presupuesto	预算
cash	dinero en efectivo	现金
cash back	recuperar el efectivo	现金返回
cashier's check	cheque de caja	出具支票
cent	centavo	分
certificate	certificado	证书
charge	cargo	收费
check	cheque	支票
checking	verificando	用支票支付
checking account	cuenta corriente	支票帐户
code	código	代号
coin	moneda	硬币
collection	recaudación	收集
conversion	conversión	转化
credit card	tarjeta de crédito	信用卡
credit card bill	factura de la tarjeta de crédito	信用卡帐单
credit rating	índice de crédito	信用等级
currency	dinero	货币

debit card, cash card
tarjeta del débito, tarjeta del dinero en efectivo
借方卡片, 现金卡片

debt	deuda	债
deferred	diferido	延期
deposit	depositar	沉积物
dime	diez centavos	一角银币
dollar	dólar	美元

down payment	pago al contado	预付定金
driver's license	licencia para manejar	驾驶执照
error	error	误差
exchange	intercambio	交换
exchange rate	tipo de cambio	交换费率
expense	gasto	费用
fees	cuotas	费用
financial planning	planificación financiera	财务计划
financial services	servicios financieros	财务服务
fixed rate	tasa fija	固定的比率
form	formulario	形式
fraud	fraude	欺骗
index	índice	索引
insufficient funds	faltas de fondos	资金不足
interest rate	tasa de interés	利率
internet banking	banca del Internet	因特网银行业
investment	inversión	投资
lease	usufructo	契约
liabilities	obligaciones	义务
limit	límite	限制
loan	préstamo	贷款
long-term	a largo plazo	长期
loss	pérdida	损失
money	dinero	钱
money market	mercado de dinero	资本市场
money order	giro postal	汇票
mortgage	hipoteca	抵押
mutual funds	fondos mutuos	公共基金
nickel	níquel	五分镍币
penalty	multa	处罚

PIN (personal identification number)
El PIN (el número de identificación personal)　个人身份号

quarter	cuarto	
real estate	bienes raíces	房地产所有权

receipt	recibo	收据
recipient	destinatario	接受者
regulation	regulación	规则
safe	seguro	安全
safety deposit box	caja fuerte	保险箱
savings	economías	积蓄
savings account	caja de ahorros	积蓄帐号
semi-annual	semi-anual	半年一次
service fee	cuota de servicio	服务费用
short-term	a corto plazo	短期
signature, sign	firma, firmar	签名
statement	declaración	协议
stock	reserva	存货
telephone bill	factura del teléfono	电话单
teller, bank clerk	cajero, empleado bancario	银行办事人员
term	término	术语
transfer	traslado	转移
traveler's cheque	cheque de viajero	旅游支票
update	actualización	更新
utility bill	factura de utilidad	工具程序帐单
value	valor	价值
variable rate	tasa variable	有效费率
wicket, window	postigo, la ventanilla	售票窗
withdraw	retirar	收回
yield	rendimiento	收益

I want to open an account.

Yo quiero abrir una cuenta. 我想开一个帐号.

I want to exchange some money.

Yo quiero intercambiar algún dinero. 我想汇一点钱.

What is the exchange rate today?

¿Cuál es el tipo de cambio hoy? 汇钱的费用是多少?

I'd like to pay my bill.

Me gustaría pagar mi factura. 我想支付我的帐单.

I'd like to make a withdrawal.

Me gustaría hacer un retiro. 我要收回我的钱.

I want to deposit my paycheck.

Yo quiero depositar mi sueldo. 我想要存我的工资支票.

May I have a receipt?

¿Puede darme un recibo? 我能有一张收据？

I want to transfer money to another account.

Yo quiero transferir el dinero a otra cuenta.
我想存钱道另一个帐号上去.

I'd like to apply for a credit card.

Me gustaría solicitar una tarjeta de crédito.
我想申请信用卡.

I want to cash this check.

Quiero cobrar este cheque. 我想要兑现这张支票.

I would like to borrow money.

Me gustaría pedir prestado el dinero. 我想借点钱.

I would like to arrange a mortgage.

Me gustaría colocar una hipoteca. 我想安排一份抵押.

Can I apply for a line of credit?

¿Yo puedo solicitar una línea de crédito? 我能申请信贷限额吗？

IDENTIFICATION	IDENTIFICACIÓN	鉴定
address	dirección	地址

apartment	apartamento	公寓
block	bloque	区域
borough	distrito municipal	自治市镇
change of address	cambio de domicilio	更换地址
child	hijo, niño	孩子
citizenship	ciudadanía	公民身份
city	ciudad	城市
civic address	dirección cívica	城市地址
civic number	número cívico	城市编号
community	comunidad	社区
country	país	国家
country of origin	país de origen	国家区域
county	condado	县
date of birth	fecha de nacimiento	生日
dependent	dependiente	依赖
document	documento	文件
driver's license	licencia para manejar	驾照
employer's name	nombre de empleador	老板的名字
family name	nombre familiar, apellido	家庭名字
first name	primer nombre	名字
given name	nombre dado	给定的名字
green card	tarjeta verde	绿卡
husband	marido	丈夫
last name	apellido	姓
middle name	segundo nombre	中间名字
name	nombre	名字
nationality	nacionalidad	国籍
neighborhood	barrio	邻居
next of kin	parientes más próximos	下次亲戚的
number	número	数字
passport	pasaporte	护照
post office box	apartado postal	邮政信箱
relative	pariente	亲戚
rural route	ruta rural	乡村道路
Social Security number	número de Seguridad social	社会保险号
spouse	esposo	配偶

street	calle	街
surname	apellido	姓
telephone number, phone	número del teléfono, teléfono	电话号码, 电话
town	pueblo	镇
unit	unidad	单位
wife	esposa	妻子
zip code	código postal	邮政编码

OCCUPATIONS / OCUPACIONES / 职业

accountant	contador	会计
administrator	administrador	管理员
apprentice	aprendiz	徒弟
architect	arquitecto	设计师
artist	artista	艺术家
associate	socio	联系
athlete	atleta	运动员
attendant	sirviente	值班员
auto mechanic	mecánico de auto	汽车
babysitter	niñera	保姆
baker	panadero	面包师
bank teller	cajero bancario	银行出纳
banker	banquero	银行家
bartender	mozo	服务员
beautician	esteticista	美容师
bell attendant	sirviente	服务员
bookkeeper	contador	薄记员
bricklayer	albañil	砖匠
broker	corredor	经纪人
bus driver	chofer del autobús	总线驱动程序
bus person	chofer del autobús	公共汽车人
businessperson	negociante, negociador	商人
carpenter	carpintero	木匠
cashier	cajero	出纳
chef	cocinero	厨师

child care worker

    trabajador en el cuidado de niños   孩子忧虑w管弦乐队

cleaner	persona que realiza limpieza	清洁工
clerk	empleado	职员
computer programmer	programador de computación	计算机程序员
concierge	portero	看门人
construction worker	obrero de la construcción	建设 工人
cook	cocinero	煮
cosmetician	cosmetóloga	美容品业者

customer service representative

    representante de servicio de cliente   顾客服务代表

customs official	funcionario de aduanas	习俗
dancer	bailarín	舞蹈演员

delivery person

persona que realiza entregas a domicilio   交货人

dental hygienist	higienista dental	牙科医生
dentist	dentista	牙医
designer	diseñador	设计者
dishwasher	lavarropas	洗碗工
doctor, physician	doctor, médico	医生
door attendant	portero	门卫
driver	chofer	司机

dry cleaner

    persona que trabaja en una tintorería   干洗工

electrician	electricista	电工
employer	empleador	老板
engineer	ingeniero	工程师
entertainer	entretenedor	招待员
entrepreneur	empresario	企业家

executive	ejecutivo	行政
farmer	granjero	农夫
fire fighter	bombero	火战士
fitness instructor	entrenador deportivo	健康教师
flight attendant	auxiliar dc vuclo	机组人员
floor supervisor	supervisor del suelo	地板监督
foreman	capataz	工头
front desk clerk	recepcionista	前台
gardener	jardinero	园丁
guide	guía	向导

| health care worker | | |
| trabajador en el cuidado de la salud | | 健康护理 |

host, hostess	arfitrión, arfitriona	主人
housekeeper	ama de casa	女管家
inspector	inspector	检查员
interpreter	intérprete	翻译
janitor	conserje	工友
jeweler	joyero	珠宝商
laborer	obrero	劳动者
laundry attendant	empleado de lavadero	洗衣员
lawyer	abogado	律师
librarian	bibliotecario	图书管理员
lifeguard	salvavidas	救生员

| loan officer | | |
| funcionario bancario (préstamos) | | 贷款官员 |

mail carrier	cartero	邮件载波
maintenance worker	obrero de mantenimiento	维修工人
manager	gerente	经理
massage therapist	masoterapeuta	按摩医师
mechanic	mecánico	技工
meteorologist	meteorólogo	气象学者
model	modelo	模型

musician	músico	音乐家
nurse	enfermera	护士
operator	operador	操作员
painter	pintor	画家
paralegal	asistente de abogados	律师助理
parole officer	oficial de libertad condicional	假释官员
photographer	fotógrafo	摄影家
physiotherapist	fisioterapeuta	理疗医师
pilot	piloto	飞行员
plant manager	gerente de la planta	厂长
plumber	plomero	管道工
police officer	agente de policía	警官
politician	político	政治家

pool attendant
    empleado de mantenimiento de pileta   水池服务员

postal worker	empleado de correo	邮政工作人员
president	presidente	总统
professor	profesor	教授
receptionist	recepcionista	接待员
repair person	técnico	修理工
reporter	reportero	记者
room attendant	mucama	空间服务员
sales representative	representante de ventas	销售代表
salesperson	vendedor	销售员
sanitation worker	obrero de higienización	卫生工作者
scientist	científico	科学家

seamstress, garment worker
    costurera   女裁缝师

secretary	secretaria	秘书
server	sirviente	服务者
singer	cantante	歌手
social worker	asistente social	社会工作者

soldier	soldado	战士
store manager	gerente de depósito	商场经理
student	estudiante	学生
subcontractor	subcontratista	转包商
supervisor	supervisor	监督人
surgeon	cirujano	外科医生
surveyor	agrimensor	检查员
tailor	sastre	裁缝
taxi driver	taxista	出租车司机
teacher	maestro	教师
teacher's aide	ayudante de maestro	助教
technician	técnico	技术员
trainee	aprendiz	新兵
translator	traductor	译员
travel agent	agente de viajes	旅行代理人
truck driver	camionero	卡车司机
veterinarian	veterinario	兽医
vice-president	vicepresidente	副总裁
waiter, waitress	mozo, camarera	服务生
window cleaner	limpiador de ventanas	窗口清洁工
worker	obrero	工人
writer	escritor	作家

COUNTRIES/NATIONALITIES — PAÍSES/NACIONALIDADES — 国家/国籍

Afghanistan, Afghan	Afganistán, afgano	阿富汗, 阿富汗人
Argentina, Argentine	Argentina, Argentino	阿根廷, 阿根廷
Bolivia, Bolivian	Bolivia, boliviano	玻利维亚
Cambodia, Cambodian	Camboya, camboyano	柬埔寨
Chile, Chilean	Chile, chileno	智利, 智利
China, Chinese	China, chino	中国, 下巴
Colombia, Columbian	Colombia, Colombiano	哥伦比亚
Costa Rica, Costa Rican	Costa Rica, costarriqueño	哥斯达黎加, 肋前缘
Cuba, Cuban	Cuba, cubano	古巴, 古巴

Dominican Republic, Dominican
República Dominicana, dominicano   多明我会共和国, 多明我会

Ecuador, Ecuadorian	Ecuador, ecuatoriano	厄瓜多尔
El Salvador, Salvadoran	El Salvador, salvadoreño	萨尔瓦多
Guatemala, Guatemalan	Guatemala, guatemalteco	危地马拉
Honduras, Honduran	Honduras, hondureño	宏都拉斯
Hong Kong, Chinese	Hong Kong, chino	香港, 汉语
India, Indian	India, hindú	印度, 印度
Indonesia, Indonesian	Indonesia, el indonesio	印度尼西亚
Japan, Japanese	Japón, japonés	日本
Laos, Laotian	Laos, el laosiano	老挝
Malaysia, Malaysian	Malasia, malasio	马来西亚
Mexico, Mexican	México, mexicano	墨西哥
Myanmar, Burmese	Myanmar, el birmano	no translation
Nicaragua, Nicaraguan	Nicaragua, nicaragüense	尼加拉瓜
Pakistan, Pakistani	Pakistán, paquistaní	巴基斯坦
Panama, Panamanian	Panamá, panameño	巴拿马
Paraguay, Paraguayan	Paraguay, paraguayo	巴拉圭
Peru, Peruvian	Perú, peruano	秘鲁
Philippines, Filipino	Filipinas, filipino	菲律宾, 菲律宾人
Puerto Rico, Puerto Rican	Puerto Rico, puertorriqueño	波多黎哥
Singapore, Singaporean	Singapur, de Singapur	no translation
South Korea, Korean	Corea del Sur, coreano	南方Kore一, 朝鲜语
Taiwan, Taiwanese	Taiwán, Taiwanés	no translation
Thailand, Thai	Tailandia, tailandés	泰国, 三趾树獭

Trinidad and Tobago, Trinidadian, Tobagonian
Trinidad y Tobago, de Trinidad y Tobago
特立尼达岛并且 Tobago, Trinidadian,   Tobagonian

United States, African-American
Estados Unidos, afro americano   统一了, 非洲-美国

United States, American
    Estados Unidos, americano   统一了, 美国

United States, Native American
    Estados Unidos, americano Nativo   统一了, 本国美国

Uruguay, Uruguayan	Uruguay, uruguayo	乌拉圭
Venezuela, Venezuelan	Venezuela, venezolano	委内瑞拉, 委内瑞拉人
Viet Nam, Vietnamese	Viet Nam, Vietnamita	越南

ACTIVITIES/RECREATION	ACTIVIDADES/RECREACIÓN	活动
aerobics	aerobics	健美操
banquet	banquete	宴会
baseball	béisbol	棒球
basketball	baloncesto	篮球
be with family	estar con la familia	和家人在一起
billiards	billar	台球
bowling	bowling	滚
cards	cartas	卡片
celebrate, celebration	celebrar, celebración	庆祝
ceremony	ceremonia	仪式
conference	conferencia	会议
dance, dancing	bailar, bailando	跳舞
date, dating	fecha, poner fecha	约会
day off	día libre	假
demonstration	demostración	在上
eat out, dine out	comer fuera, cenar fuera	外面吃, 喧嚣外面
event	evento	事件
exercise	ejercicio	锻练
fishing	pesca	钓鱼
football	fútbol	足球
go camping	acampar	去宿营
go climbing	escalar	去爬
go for a drive	paseo en auto	开车

go for coffee	tomar un café	去咖啡
go sailing	navegar	走航行
go shopping, shop	ir de compras, la tienda	买东西, 商店
go sightseeing	ir de turismo	走
go to a bar	ir a un bar	去一间酒吧
go to a concert	ir a un concierto	去反对确实事件
go to a game	ira un juego	玩游戏
go to a movie	ir a ver una película	看电影
go to a museum	ir a un museo	去一亩
go to a restaurant	ir a un restaurante	去休息
go to a show/play	ir a un show/partido	去一/游戏
go to an art gallery	ir a una galería de arte	去艺术画廊
go to the mall	ir al centro comercial	去m所有
golf	golf	高尔夫
gymnasium	gimnasio	体育馆
gymnastics	gimnasias	体操
hang out	andar	外面挂
have a drink	tomar algo	喝一杯
have a picnic	hacer pic nic	有一
have dinner	tener una cena	吃晚饭
have lunch	almorzar	吃午餐
hockey	hockey	曲棍球
invite over, out	invitar	邀请过去
jogging	trotar	慢跑
lacrosse	lacrosse	长内棍球
listen to music	escuchar música	听亩原文如此
match	juego, partido	火柴
meeting	reunión	会议
parade	desfile	游行
party, to party	fiesta	宴会, 到平等
performance	espectáculo	表现
picnic	pic nic	野餐
play	jugar	玩
play (music)	tocar/hacer (la música)	玩 (音乐)
play sports	hacer deportes	打运动
playground	patio de recreo	运动场

pool	piscina	水池
practice	practicar	实践
program	programa	节目
read, reading	leer, leyendo	读, 写入
reception	recepción	接收
relax	descansar	放松
rest	descansar	休息
rink	pista de patinar	溜冰场
run, running	correr, corriendo	跑, 跑
show	show	出现
shower	ducha	淋浴
sing, singing	cantar, cantando	唱歌
skating	patinando	溜冰
skiing	esquiando	滑雪
sleep, sleep in	dormir, dormir en	睡觉
soccer	fútbol	足球
sports	deportes	运动
stadium	estadio	体育场
swim, swimming	nadar, nadando	游泳
tennis	tenis	网球
time off	tiempo fuera de	时间离开
tribute	tributo	献礼
vacation	vacación	假期
volleyball	voleibol	排球
volunteer	voluntario	志愿者
walk, walking	caminar, caminando	步行
watch television	mirar la televisión	看电视
wedding	casamiento	婚礼
weekend	fin de semana	周末
Do you like to ____?	¿Le gusta ____?	你喜欢吗?
Do you play _____?	¿Usted juega _____?	你玩...?
Shall we...?	¿Podemos...?	我们会...?
Would you like to...?	¿Le gustaría ...?	你喜欢吗?
Can I buy you a drink?	¿Quiere una bebida?	我买饮料你喝好吗?
Are you busy?	¿ Está ocupado?	你忙吗?
Are you available?	¿Usted está disponible?	你有空吗?

Do you have plans?	¿ Tiene planes?	我有计划吗？
Sorry, I am busy.	Discúlpeme, estoy ocupado.	对不起，我很忙．
I have other plans.	Yo tengo otros planes.	我有其他计划．
I have to work.	Yo tengo que trabajar.	我必须工作．
Maybe another time.	Quizás en otro momento.	其他时间吧．
I would like that.	Me gustaría eso.	我喜欢那．

What time shall we meet?

¿A qué hora nosotros nos encontraremos?   我们什么时间会面？

Shall I pick you up?	¿Los paso a buscar?	我能认识你吗？
Where do you live?	¿Dónde vive Ud?	你生活在那里？
I will meet you there.	Yo lo encontraré allí.	我会在那里见到你
See you then.	Véalo entonces.	再见．
Can I call you?	¿Puedo llamarlo?	我能叫你吗？

Can I have your telephone number?

¿Me puede dar su número del teléfono?   我能有你的电话号码吗？

EMERGENCIES   EMERGENCIAS   紧急事件

accident	accidente	事故
alarm	alarma	警报
AR (artificial respiration)	RA (la respiración artificial)	人造 呼吸
bleeding	sangrando	流血
candle	vela	蜡烛
choking	ahogando	阻塞
clinic	clínica	诊所
convulsion	convulsión	惊厥

CPR (cardiopulmonary resuscitation)

CPR (la resurrección cardiopulmonar)   no translation

dehydration	deshidratación	脱水
dispatcher	distribuidor	发送者

earthquake	terremoto	地震
emergency services	servicios de emergencia	紧急情况服务
evacuation plan	plan de la evacuación	撤退计划
fire department	departamento de incendios	消防部门
fire engine	máquinas contra incendios	火引擎
fire extinguisher	extintor de incendios	灭火器
fire hydrant	boca de incendios	火给水栓
first aid	primeros auxilios	急救
first aid kit	equipo de primeros auxilios	急救工具包
flare	señal luminosa	闪光
flashlight	linterna eléctrica	闪亮
flood	diluvio	洪水
generator	generador	发电机
hospital	hospital	医院
hurricane	huracán	飓风
lightning	relámpago	闪电
matches	fósforos	火柴
next-of-kin	familiar más cercano	至亲
operator	operador	操作员
outpatient	enfermo ambulatorio	门诊病人
overdose	dosis excesiva	配药量过多
paramedic	paramédico	伞兵军医

Poison Control Centre
    Centro de Verificación de Veneno   病毒控制中心

poisoning	envenenando	毒害
police	policía	警察
rape	violación	强奸
rescue	rescate	救
safety manual	manual de seguridad	安全手册
search and rescue	búsqueda y rescate	搜索并且救
seizure	ataque	抓住
shelter	resguardo	掩蔽
shock	susto	吃惊
smoke detector	detector de humo	烟

storm	tormenta	暴风雨
tornado	tornado	旋风
tow truck	grúa remolque	拖车
toxic	tóxico	有毒
trauma	trauma	损伤
X-ray	radiografía	射线
Call 911!	¡Llame al 911!	叫911！
Don't use the elevator.	No use el ascensor.	不要使用电梯.
Fire!	¡Fuego!	火！
Get down!	¡Baje!	下去！
Get under the table!	¡Resguárdese bajo la mesa!	到桌子底下去！
Go outside!	¡Vaya fuera!	在外面走！
Help!	¡Ayuda!	帮助！
Hurry!	¡Dé prisa!	赶紧！

I am having a heart attack.

Yo estoy teniendo un ataque cardíaco.

.我正在有一次心脏病发作.

Please call an ambulance.

Por favor llame una ambulancia. 请打电话叫一辆救护车.

Stay away from the windows!

¡Apártese de las ventanas! 从窗户处离开！

There's been an accident.

Hay un accidente. 已经发生了一次事故.

I can't breathe.	Yo no puedo respirar.	我不能呼吸.
I need a doctor.	Yo necesito a un doctor.	我需要一个医生.
I've been robbed.	Me han robado.	我已经被抢劫.
Security!	¡Policía!	安全！
She's/He's unconscious.	Él/Ella esta inconsciente.	她/他是无意识.
Someone is choking.	Alguien se está ahogando.	某人是 阻塞.
Someone is sick.	Alguien está enfermo.	某人在 生病.
Watch out!	¡Tenga cuidado!	提防！

MEDICAL TERMS	TÉRMINOS MEDICOS	医药的
AIDS	SIDA	帮助
allergy	alergia	过敏症
backache	dolor de espalda	背痛
bandage	venda	绷带
beneficiary	beneficiario	受益人
blister	ampolla	水泡
blood type	grupo sanguíneo	血类型
blood, blood test	sangre, análisis de sangre	血,血 测试
broken	quebrado	碎
bruise	moretón	伤痕
burned	quemado	烧
cancer	cáncer	癌
cane	bastón	藤条
cast	yeso	扔
check-up	control médico	检查
claim form	libro de quejas	声称形式
claimant	demandante	提出要求者
contact lens	lentes de contacto	接触透镜
contagious	contagioso	感染
co-pay amount	pago compartido	付
cough	tos	咳嗽
cough syrup	jarabe de la tos	咳嗽果汁
coverage	cobertura	覆盖
cramp	calambre	痉挛
cream	crema	乳脂
crutches	muletas	丁字拐
decongestant	descongestionante	解充血药
deductible	deducible	可减除
dependent	dependiente	依赖
depression	depresión	消沉
dizziness	vértigo	头昏
examination	examen	检查
faint	desmáyese	微弱
family policy	política familiar	家庭政策

fever	fiebre	发烧
flu	gripe	流行感冒
glasses	anteojos	杯子
group insurance	seguro de grupo	团体保险
head cold	resfriado	领导冷
headache	dolor de cabeza	头疼
health plan	plan de salud	健康计划
hearing aid	audífono	助听器
heart disease	enfermedad del corazón	心脏病
infected	infectado	感染
inoculation	inoculación	接种
insurance card	tarjeta de seguro	保险卡
insurance company	compañía de seguros	保险公司
medication	medicación	药物
medicine	medicina	药
nausea	náusea	作呕
needle	aguja	针
nurse	enfermera	护士
office visit	visita de oficina	办公访问
pain	dolor	疼痛
patient	paciente	病人
penicillin	penicilina	青霉素
pharmacist	farmacéutico	药剂师
pharmacy	farmacia	药学
physical	físico	物理
physician	médico	医生
pills	píldoras	药丸
pregnant	embarazada	孕育
premium	premio	奖赏
prescription	prescripción	药方
rash	salpullido	皮疹
release form	formulario de alta médica	版本形式
shot	tiro	射击
sick	enfermo	生病
sneeze	estornudo	喷嚏
sore	herida	酸

specialist	especialista	专家
sprained	torcido	扭伤
stitches	puntadas	缝针
stomachache	dolor de barriga	胃痛
stress	stress	压力
surgeon	cirujano	外科医生
surgery	cirugía	手术
swollen	hinchado	肿胀
thermometer	termómetro	温度计
toothache	dolor de muelas	牙痛
treatment	tratamiento	待遇
twisted	torcido	捻
ulcer	úlcera	腐烂物
veterinarian	veterinario	兽医
vomiting	vomitando	呕吐
waiting room	sala dc espera	等后室
wheelchair	silla de ruedas	轮椅

Need a Quick Reference?

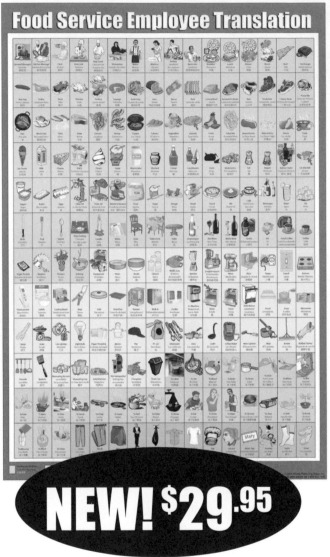

Food Service Employee Translation

NEW! KEY WORDS FOOD SERVICE EMPLOYEE TRANSLATION POSTER

Atlantic Publishing's bilingual food service key words poster is the perfect solution for getting your message across to non-English-speaking employees. These attractive and colorful posters detail a four-color picture of the food service item, such as a knife, thermometer, loaf of bread, etc., and provide the English, Spanish and Chinese translation. As a manager, you can simply point to the item while trying to learn and pronounce the translation. At the same time, the employees will have a training aid to begin to learn the English language. Also, Spanish- and Chinese-speaking employees will be able to begin to communicate in their native dialects. Posters are laminated to reduce wear and tear and measure 17" x 25".

To order call 800-541-1336 or visit www.atlantic-pub.com
Item #KWF-PS $29.95

ENDNOTES

& SOURCES

1. U.S. Census Bureau, *Statistical Abstract of the United States: 2001*, 13; <http://www.census.gov/prod/2002pubs/01statab/pop.pdf>.

2. Robert Bernstein and Mike Bergman, *"Hispanic Population Reaches All-Time High of 38.8 Million, New Census Bureau Estimates Show,"* (Washington, D.C.: U.S. Census Bureau, Public Information Office press release, <http://www.census.gov/Press-Release/www/2003/cb03-100.html>, June 18, 2003.

3. The U.S. Employment Equal Opportunity Commission, *"National Origin Discrimination"* [updated January 14, 2004]; <http://www.eeoc.gov/origin/index.html>.

4. National Immigration Law Center, *"Immigrants, Employment and Public Benefits"* (Los Angeles, 2003); <http://www.nilc.org/immspbs/research/factsaboutimms.htm>.

5. Roberto Ramirez and G. Patricia de la Cruz, *The Hispanic Population in the United States: March 2002* (Washington, D.C.: US Census Bureau, Current Population Reports, 2002), P20-545; <http://www.census.gov/population/www/socdemo/hispanic/ho02.html>.

6. Bernadette D. Proctor and Joseph Dalaker, *Poverty in the United States: 2002* (Washington, D.C.: U.S. Census Bureau, Current Population Reports, 2003), P60-222; <http://www

.census.gov/prod/2003pubs/p60-222/pdf>.

7. Terrance Reeves and Claudette Bennett, *The Asian and Pacific Islander Population in the United States: March 2002* (Washington, D.C.: U.S. Census Bureau, Current Population Reports, 2003), P20-540; <http://www.census.gov /population/www/socdemo/race/api.html>.

8. Katharine Esty, Richard Griffin and Marcie Schorr Hirsch, *Workplace Diversity: A Manager's Guide to Solving Problems and Turning Diversity into a Competitive Advantage* (Massachusetts: Adams Media Corporation, 1995), 9-11.

9. The U.S. Employment Equal Opportunity Commission, *"Other Discriminatory Practices under EEO Laws"* [updated August 13, 2003]; <http://www.eeoc.gov/abouteeo/overview_practices .html>.

10. The U.S. Employment Equal Opportunity Commission, *"Federal Laws Prohibiting Job Discrimination Questions and Answers,"* [updated May 24, 2002]; <http://www.eeoc.gov /facts/qanda.html>.

11. Loc. cit. (EEOC).

12. State of New Jersey, *"Certified Target Areas under the Immigration Act of 1990,"* <http://www.state.nj.us/njbiz/r _cert_target.shtml>.

13. "DREAM Act Reintroduced in Senate, *"Immigrants' Rights Update,* Vol. 17, No. 5 (September 4, 2003); <http://www.nilc .org/immlawpolicy/DREAM/Dream001.htm>.

14. Michael Liedtke, *"Wal-Mart Says Sex Discrimination Lawsuit Should Be Dismantled,"* (Associated Press, September 26, 2003); <http://www.imdiversity.com/Article_Detail .asp?Article_ID=19770>.

15. Colin Moynihan, *"Latino Police Officers and City Settle Suit"* (The New York Times, February 1, 2004); <http://www .policeone.com>.

16. Page Ivey, *"Denny's chain moves past lawsuit, buries racist past"* [online] (Associated Press, The Detroit News, April 19, 2002); available from http://www.detnews.2002 /business/0204/09/b04-460284.htm; INTERNET.

17. Fay Hansen, *"Diversity's Business Case Doesn't Add Up,"* Workforce Management (April 2003); <http:www.workforce .com/section/11feature/23/42/49>.

18. Linda Bean, *"What Went Wrong with the MIT-Led Diversity Study—And Why It Was Misinterpreted,"* DiversityInc., December 2003/January 2004, 38-40.

19. Riccardo A. Davis, *"Year of the Asian American: Banks See Enormous Potential in 2004,"* DiversityInc., December 2003/ January 2004, 103-4.

20. Yoji Cole, *"Automakers Get the Point: Reach Customers in their Own Spaces,"* DiversityInc., December 2003/January 2004, 107.

21. George Simons and Amy J. Zuckerman, *"Working Together: Succeeding in a Multicultural Organization,"* Revised ed. (Menlo Park, California: Crisp Publications, Inc., 1994), 7.

22. Simons, 15.

23. C.N. Le, *"Socioeconomic Statistics & Demographics,"* Asian-Nation: The Landscape of Asian America, (Amherst, Massachusetts, February 7, 2004); <http://www.asian-nation.org/demographics.shtml.

24. Le.

25. Jennifer Parker Talwar, *"Fast Food, Fast Track: Immigrants, Big Business and the American Dream"* (Boulder, Colorado: Westview Press, 2002), 75.

26. Parker Talwar, 125.

27. Parker Talwar, 123.

28. Stella Ting-Toomey, *"Intercultural Conflict Management: A Mindful Approach"* excerpted from Ting-Toomey's *Communicating Across Cultures* (New York: The Guildford Press, 1999), 194-230; <www.personal.anderson.ucla.edu/richard.goodman/c4web/mindful.htm>.

29. Scott D. Seligman, *"Chinese Business Etiquette: A Guide to Protocol, Manner, and Culture in the People's Republic of China"* (New York: Warner Books, Inc., 1999) 31-33.

30. Jennifer Thomas, *"Spanish for Hospitality and Food Service"* (Upper Saddle River, New Jersey: Pearson Prentice Hall, 2004), 242.

31. Vadim Kotelnikov, *Ten3 Business e-Coach* (Moscow); <http://1000ventures.com/business_guide/crosscuttings/leadership_main.html>.

32. Courtland L. Bovée and John V. Thill, *"Business Communication Today,"* 6th ed. (Upper Saddle River, New Jersey: Prentice Hall, 2000), 64.

33. Thomas Vulpe, Director of the Centre for Intercultural Learning, a branch of Canada's Department of Foreign Affairs, discussing required skills for successful intercultural communication. *"Sounds Like Canada,"* radio interview with Shelagh Rogers (Toronto: Canadian Broadcasting Corporation, March 8, 2004).

34. Bovée, 68.

35. Seligman, 14.

36. Seligman, 201.

37. Doug Whalen and K. David Harrison. *"The World's Endangered Languages,"* Encarta Yearbook (Microsoft, Feb. 2000) [CD-ROM].

38. Richard L. Weaver II, *Understanding Interpersonal Communication,* 5th ed. (Bowling Green State University: HarperCollins, 1990), 167.

39. Kotelnikov.

40. Robert T. Carroll, *"The Skeptic's Dictionary"* (Sacramento, CA, 2002); <http://www.skepdic.com/neurolin.html>.

41. Christopher Heffner, *"Communication Styles,"* (Carbondale, IL, 2003); <http://www.siu.edu/offices/counsel/talk.htm>.

42. Simons, 37.

43. Weaver, 132.

44. Weaver, 147.

45. Maxwell, John C., *"Developing the Leaders Around You"* (Nashville: Thomas Nelson, Inc., 1995), 98-101.

46. Thomas, 189.

47. Seligman, 174, 176.

48. Jim Shaffer, *"The Leadership Solution"* (New York: McGraw-Hill, 2000), 35.

49. Weaver, 325.

50. Seligman, 86.

51. Lenora Billings-Harris, *"The Diversity Advantage: A Guide to Making Diversity Work"* (Greensboro, NC: Oakhill Press, 1998), 114.

52. R. Roosevelt Thomas, *"Beyond Race and Gender: Unleashing the Power of Your Total Workforce by Managing Diversity"* (New York: American Management Association, 1991), 10, 12.

Sources

Books:

Adams, Bob et al., *Managing People: Lead Your Staff to Peak Performance*, Adams Media Corporation, Holbrook, MA, 1998.

Association for Japanese-Language Teaching, *Japanese for Busy People*, Kodansha International, Tokyo, 1988.

Billings-Harris, Lenora, *The Diversity Advantage: A Guide to Making Diversity Work*, Oakhill Press, Greensboro, NC, 1998.

Bovée, Courtland L. and John V. Thill, *Business Communication Today*, 6th ed., Prentice Hall, Upper Saddle River, New Jersey, 2000.

Briscoe, Dennis R., *International Human Resource Management*, Prentice Hall, Englewood Cliffs, New Jersey, 1995.

Casado, Matt A., *Conversational Spanish for Hospitality Managers & Supervisors*, John Wiley & Sons, Inc., New York, 1995.

Conference of Local Authorities for International Relations, *Japanese Language Text*, *Book One*, CLAIR, Tokyo, 1987.

D'Aprix, David, *International Foreign Language Guide for Hotel Employees*, Living Language (a Random House company), New York, 1998.

Esty, Katharine, Richard Griffin and Marcie Schorr Hirsch, *Workplace Diversity: A Manager's Guide to Solving Problems and Turning Diversity into a Competitive Advantage*, Adams Media

Corporation, Massachusetts, 1995.

Gómez-Mejía, Luis R., David B. Balkin and Robert L. Cardy, *Managing Human Resources*, 3rd ed., Prentice Hall, Upper Saddle River, New Jersey, 2001.

Gootnick, David E. and Margaret Mary Gootnick, Eds, *The Standard Handbook of Business Communication*, The Free Press, New York, 1984.

Harvey, William C., *Spanish for Human Resources Managers*, Barron's Educational Series, Inc., New York, 1997.

Kelly, George W. and Rex R. Kelly, *Spanish for the Housewife*, Vanderpool, Texas, The Kelly Brothers (self-published), 1973.

Maxwell, John C., *Developing the Leaders Around You*, Thomas Nelson Publishers, Nashville, 1995.

Parker Talwar, Jennifer, *Fast Food, Fast Track: Immigrants, Big Business and the American Dream*, Westview Press, Boulder, Colorado, 2002.

Seligman, Scott D., *Chinese Business Etiquette: A Guide to Protocol, Manner, and Culture in the People's Republic of China*, Warner Books, Inc., New York, 1999.

Simons, George and Amy J. Zuckerman, *Working Together: Succeeding in a Multicultural Organization*, Revised ed., Crisp Publications, Inc., Menlo Park, California, 1994.

Shaffer, Jim, *The Leadership Solution*, McGraw-Hill, New York, 2000.

Thomas, Jennifer, *Spanish for Hospitality & Foodservice*, Pearson

Prentice Hall, Upper Saddle River, New Jersey, 2004.

Thomas, R. Roosevelt Jr., *Beyond Race and Gender: Unleashing the Power of Your Total Workforce for Managing Diversity*, AMACOM (American Management Association), New York, 1991.

Weaver, Richard L. II, *Understanding Interpersonal Communication*, 5th ed., HarperCollins, Bowling Green State University, 1990.

Zachary, G. Pascal, *The Global Me: New Cosmopolitans and the Competitive Edge: Picking Globalism's Winners and Losers*, Public Affairs, New York, 2000.

Internet:

U.S. Census Bureau, *Statistical Abstract of the United States: 2001*; <http://www.census.gov/prod/2002pubs/01statab/pop.pdf>.

CIA Word Factbook, Washington, D.C., 2003 [updated December 13, 2003]; <http://www.cia.gov/cia/publications/factbook/geos /kn.html>.

Equal Employment Opportunity Commission. "National Origin Discrimination"; updated January 14, 2003]; < http://www.eeoc .gov>.

Latin America Network Information Centre, University of Texas at Austin, 2004; <http://lanic.utexas.edu/la/region/hispanic>.

Kotelnikov, Vadim; *Ten3 - the Business e-Coach*, Moscow; <http: //www.1000ventures.com/business_guide/crosscuttings /leadership_main.html>.

Carroll, Robert T., *The Skeptic's Dictionary*, Sacramento, CA, 2002; < http://www.skepdic.com/neurolin.html>.

Bernstein, Robert and Mike Bergman, *"Hispanic Population Reaches All-Time High of 38.8 Million, New Census Bureau Estimates Show,"* Washington, D.C.: U.S. Census Bureau Public Information Office (press release), June 18, 2003; < http://www.census.govPress -Release/www/2003/cb03-100.html>.

Hansen, Fay, *"Diversity's Business Case Doesn't Add Up,"* Workforce Management, April 2003; <http://www.workforce.com/section/11 /feature/23/42/49>.

Heffner, Christopher, *"Communication Styles,"* Carbondale, IL, Southern Illinois University, 2003; <http://www.siu.edu/offices /counsel/talk.htm>.

Ivey, Page. *"Denny's Chain Moves Past Lawsuit, Buries Racist Past,"* The Detroit News, Detroit, April 19, 2002; <http://www.detnews .com/2002/business/0204/09/b04-460284.htm>.

Le, C. N., *"Socioeconomic Statistics & Demographics,"* Asian-Nation: The Landscape of Asian America, Amherst, Massachusetts, February 7, 2004; <http://www.asian-nation.org/demographics. shtml>.

Liedtke, Michael, *"Wal-Mart Says Sex Discrimination Lawsuit Should be Dismantled,"* Associated Press, September 26, 2003; <http: //www.IMdiversity.com/Article_Detail.asp?Article_ID=19770>.

Moynihan, Colin, *"Latino NYPD Officers and City Settle Suit,"* The New York Times, February 1, 2004; <http://www.policeone.com>.

Proctor, Bernadette D. and Joseph Dalaker, *"Poverty in the United States: 2002,"* Washington, D.C: U.S. Census Bureau, Current

Population Reports, 2003, P60-222; <http://www.census.gov/prod /2003pubs/p60-222.pdf>.

Ramirez, Roberto R. and G. Patricia de la Cruz, *"The Hispanic Population in the United States: March 2002,"* Washington, D.C.: U.S. Census Bureau, Current Population Reports, June 2003, P20-545; <http://www.census.gov/population/www/socdemo/hispanic /ho02.html>.

Reeves, Terrance and Claudette Bennett, *"The Asian and Pacific Islander Population in the United States: March 2002,"* Washington, D.C.: U.S. Census Bureau, Current Population Reports, May 2003, P20-540; <http://www.census.gov/population/www/socdemo /race/api.html>.

Schmidley, Dianne, *"The Foreign-born Population in the United States: March 2002,"* Washington, D.C.: U.S. Census Bureau, Current Population Reports, 2003, P20-539; <http://www.census .gov/prod/2003pubs/p20-539.pdf>.

Ting-Toomey, Stella. *"Intercultural Conflict Management: A Mindful Approach,"* excerpted from Ting-Toomey's Communicating Across Cultures, New York: The Guildford Press, 1999, 194-230; <http: //www.personal.anderson.ucla.edu/richard.goodman/c4web /mindful.htm>.

Quotations:

<http://www.wisdomquotes.com>

<http://www.cybernation.com/victory/quotations/subjects /quotes_communication.html>

<http://www.dailycelebrations.com/../communication.htm>

<http://parallel.park.uga.edu/~tengles/102m/concepts.html>

<http://www.quotesandsayings.com>

<http://www.theotherpages.org>

Periodicals:

Communication Briefings: Ideas that Work, Vol. XXII, No. 1 (Preview Issue), Georgetown Publishing Group, Alexandria, Virginia, February 10, 2004.

DiversityInc. Vol. 2, Number 6, New Brunswick, NJ, December 2003/January 2004.

McCarthy, Shawn, *"38 Million Hispanics Worth Wooing,"* The Globe and Mail, March 29, 2004, sec. B, 1, 4.

CD-ROM:

Whalen, Doug and K. David Harrison, *"The World's Endangered Languages,"* Encarta Yearbook, Microsoft, February 2000.

Radio Program:

Thomas Vulpe, Director of the Centre for Intercultural Learning, a branch of Canada's Department of Foreign Affairs; radio interview with Shelagh Rogers. Canadian Broadcasting Corporation, Toronto, March 8, 2004.

Good Employees Are the Key to Success

Ask any manager today and they'll say their biggest concern is the competition for talented, good employees. The business costs and impact of employee turnover can be grouped into four major categories: costs resulting from a person leaving, hiring costs, training costs, and lost productivity costs. The estimated cost to replace an employee is at least 150 percent of the person's base salary. As you can see, managers must learn to hire, train and keep employees highly motivated.

Every organization needs a system for hiring, training and keeping superb employees, and that is exactly what you'll get from this new book. You will learn to create a workplace full of self-motivated employees who are highly purpose-driven.

You will learn the fundamentals of sound hiring, how to identify high-performance candidates, and how to spot evasions and even lies. This book contains a wide assortment of carefully worded questions that help make the process more effective. Innovative step-by-step descriptions of how to recruit, interview, hire, train and KEEP the best people for every position in your organization.

This book is filled to the brim with innovative and fun training ideas (that cost little or nothing) and ideas for increasing employee involvement and enthusiasm. When you get your employees involved and enthused, you will keep them interested and working with you, not against you. With the help of this book, get started today on building your workplace into one that inspires employees to do excellent work because they really want to!

Numerous case studies and examples show how you can create an environment in which employees feel passionate about their jobs. The companion CD-ROM contains dozens of employee training and human resource forms including: unique employment applications, interview questions and analysis, reference checks, work schedules, rules to live by, reporting forms, confidentially agreement, and an extensive human resource audit form. Simply print out any form you need, when you need it.

INDEX

We recently lost our beloved pet "Bear," who was not only our best and dearest friend but also the "Vice President of Sunshine" here at Atlantic Publishing. He did not receive a salary but worked tirelessly 24 hours a day to please his parents. Bear was a rescue dog that turned around and showered myself, my wife Sherri, his grandparents Jean, Bob and Nancy and every person and animal he met (maybe not rabbits) with friendship and love. He made a lot of people smile every day.

We wanted you to know that a portion of the profits of this book will be donated to The Humane Society of the United States.

–Douglas & Sherri Brown

THE HUMANE SOCIETY
OF THE UNITED STATES ©

The human-animal bond is as old as human history. We cherish our animal companions for their unconditional affection and acceptance. We feel a thrill when we glimpse wild creatures in their natural habitat or in our own backyard.

Unfortunately, the human-animal bond has at times been weakened. Humans have exploited some animal species to the point of extinction.

The Humane Society of the United States makes a difference in the lives of animals here at home and worldwide. The HSUS is dedicated to creating a world where our relationship with animals is guided by compassion. We seek a truly humane society in which animals are respected for their intrinsic value, and where the human-animal bond is strong.

Want to help animals? We have plenty of suggestions. Adopt a pet from a local shelter, join The Humane Society and be a part of our work to help companion animals and wildlife. You will be funding our educational, legislative, investigative and outreach projects in the U.S. and across the globe.

Or perhaps you'd like to make a memorial donation in honor of a pet, friend or relative? You can through our Kindred Spirits program. And if you'd like to contribute in a more structured way, our Planned Giving Office has suggestions about estate planning, annuities, and even gifts of stock that avoid capital gains taxes.

Maybe you have land that you would like to preserve as a lasting habitat for wildlife. Our Wildlife Land Trust can help you. Perhaps the land you want to share is a backyard—that's enough. Our Urban Wildlife Sanctuary Program will show you how to create a habitat for your wild neighbors.

So you see, it's easy to help animals. And The HSUS is here to help.

The Humane Society of the United States
2100 L Street NW
Washington, DC 20037
202-452-1100
www.hsus.org